FLOWERING
TREES
&
SHRUBS

GARDENERS' POCKET PICTURE GUIDES

FLOWERING TREES & SHRUBS

BRIAN DAVIS

Rodale Press, Emmaus, Pennsylvania

Designed and produced by
Breslich & Foss
Golden House
28-31 Great Pulteney Street
London W1R 3DD

Project Editor: Judy Martin
Editor: Jim Abram
Designer: Roger Daniels
Paste-up Artist: Elly King

Published in 1988 in the
United States of America by
Rodale Press, Inc
33 E. Minor St.
Emmaus, PA 18098

ISBN 0-87857-745-9 Paperback

Printed and bound in Hong Kong
by Mandarin Offset

INTRODUCTION

Every year new varieties of flowering trees and
shrubs are introduced to plant catalogues and
garden centres. The sheer generosity of choice is
enough to bewilder the most informed and dis-
cerning gardener. For this pocket guide I have
selected 450 of the finest, including many varieties
of established popularity and others less familiar
but equally deserving of attention.

The selection covers the full range of flower
colours, shapes and sizes, and the inclusion of both
trees and shrubs ensures that you can create a
single specimen or featured planting precisely
suited to the available space and conditions in your
garden. Entries arranged alphabetically provide
full details of care and cultivation, and illustrations
show both the overall shape of the tree or shrub
and the splendour of its appearance in flower. A
description of each variety enables you to select
other attractive features, such as ornamental bark
or autumn foliage colour, and explains special uses
such as screening or patio planting which you may
wish to take into account in your garden scheme.

This book is designed to answer the questions
you would wish to ask about not only the most
beautiful, but also the most suitable flowering
trees and shrubs for your garden. I hope you will
enjoy using it to select your plants, as much as you
will enjoy the fabulous display of colour in your
garden in the seasons to come.

BRIAN DAVIS

AMELANCHIER CANADENSIS
(Amelanchier lamarckii)

SHADBLOW SERVICEBERRY, SNOWY MESPILUS
Rosaceae
Deciduous
An attractive small tree for all sizes of garden.

Origin From North America and Canada, and now naturalized throughout most of Europe. Commonly sold in Europe and the UK as *A. lamarckii.*

Amelanchier canadensis **in flower**

Use Grown as a standard tree to make a featured specimen for small, medium or large gardens.

Description *Flower* Racemes of white flowers produced in late spring, before or just after leaves appear. *Foliage* Leaves ovate, 2-3in (5-8cm) long, light green with slight orange-red veining and shading on some soil conditions. Brilliant orange-red autumn colours. *Stem* Strong, upright when young, becoming twiggy and arching with age. Often grown as a large shrub, but readily produces a single trunk to form a small round-headed tree. Medium rate of growth. *Fruit* Small, light red fruits produced in racemes in autumn. Degree of fruiting dependent on the heat and dryness of summer.

Hardiness Tolerates winter temperatures below $-13°F$ ($-25°C$).

Soil Requirements Any soil type; tolerates alkalinity and acidity.

Sun/Shade aspect Best in full sun, but tolerates quite deep shade.

Pruning None required, but any lower shoots or branches may be removed.

Propagation and nursery production From layers or by removal of a sucker from the base. On bushy plants up to 2ft (60cm) a single stem may be encouraged to develop by

Average height and spread
Five years
14½x10ft (4.5x3m)
Ten years
22x16ft (6.5x5m)
Twenty years or at maturity
25x20ft (7.5x6m)

pruning. Trees pretrained up to 6-10ft (2-3m) are available. Plant bare-rooted or container-grown. Relatively easy to find in production.

Problems When grown as a standard tree is sometimes grafted on to *Crataegus oxyacantha* or *Pyrus communis*. Both these forms can be poor-rooted and produce suckers which must be removed.

Varieties of interest *A. laevis* Oval foliage producing good autumn colours. Branches more open and flowers more widely spaced, but larger individual flowers per open raceme. From eastern North America.

BERBERIS DARWINII

DARWIN'S BARBERRY
Berberidaceae
Evergreen
A very fine spring-flowering shrub as long as the right conditions can be given.

Origin From Chile and Argentina. First discovered by the naturalist Charles Darwin, from whom it takes its name, on the voyage of the 'Beagle' in 1835.

Use As a spring-flowering evergreen for shrub borders or for mass planting. Plant 2½ft (80cm) apart in single line for informal hedge.

Description *Flower* Bright orange, hanging, double, cup-shaped flowers borne in clusters on wood 2 years old or more in great profusion in early to mid spring. *Foliage* Leaves ovate, ½-1in (1-3cm) long, with five-pointed edges, olive green upper surfaces, silver undersides. Although evergreen some of the leaves of very old branches may turn red in autumn when old leaves are discarded. *Stem* Light to mid green, aging to green-brown. Strong, upright when young, becoming spreading and twiggy with age. Small spines, flexible when young, at most leaf and stem axils, which become woody with age. Medium growth rate. *Fruit* Clusters of blue-black hanging fruits on mature wood in autumn.

Hardiness Unlikely to survive temperatures below 14°F (−10°C). Young new growth may be damaged by late spring frosts, but without lasting effect.

Soil Requirements Does well in most, but dislikes thin, chalk soils or very dry areas.

Sun/Shade aspect Prefers light dappled shade, tolerates sun or shade.

Pruning On mature shrubs remove some wood 3-4 years old to ground level each spring to encourage rejuvenation. After hard spring pruning flowering will be reduced during the 2-3 years it takes to rejuvenate.

Propagation and nursery production From cuttings taken in midsummer. Buy plants raised from cuttings as seed-raised stock can be very variable. Plant container-grown. Available from garden centres and general nurseries. Best planting heights 15in-2½ft (40-80cm).

Problems Whole mature plants, or sections may die very suddenly in summer, perhaps

Average height and spread
Five years
5x5ft (1.5x1.5m)
Ten years
7x6ft (2.2x2m)
Twenty years or at maturity
10x10ft (3x3m)

due to damage to roots by drying out or waterlogging but the reason is not fully understood.

Berberis darwinii **in flower**

BERBERIS × STENOPHYLLA

KNOWN BY BOTANICAL NAME
Berberidaceae
Evergreen
A useful range of evergreen, spring-flowering shrubs, offering a wide variation in height and habit.

Origin Of garden origin, with *B. darwinii* in its parentage.

Use As a single, spring-flowering shrub for the shrub border, for mass planting or, if planted 3ft (1m) apart in a single line, for an informal hedge.

Description *Flower* Yellow, double, cup-shaped, flowers hanging singly and in threes along arching branches, early to late spring. *Foliage* Leaves narrow, lanceolate, convexed, curving, ½-1in (1-3cm) long, olive green upper surfaces, silver-white undersides. *Stem* Light to bright green when young, aging to dark green and brown. Single or triple thorns at each leaf axil. Upright, becoming spreading and gracefully arching, forming large mound of equal height and spread. Some growth can occur at ground level, with shoots arising from underground stolons. Medium to fast growth rate. *Fruit* Small, oblong, blue to blue-black fruit borne freely along branches in some hot summers.

Hardiness Tolerates 4°F (−15°C) but winter wind chill may damage foliage.

Soil Requirements Does well on most, but unhappy on very dry or thin chalk soils.

Sun/Shade aspect Full sun to heavy deep shade.

Pruning If cut to ground level will rejuvenate

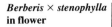

in 2-3 years. May be clipped very hard when used as hedge.

Propagation and nursery production From cuttings taken in summer. Purchase container-grown; widely available. Best planting heights 1-2½ft (30-80cm).

Problems May be slow to establish.

Varieties of interest *B.* × *stenophylla 'Autumnalis'* Produces a second crop of flowers in autumn'. A slower growing variety, attaining two-thirds the height and spread of its parent. *B.* × *s.* *'Claret Cascade'* Arching purple-red branches carry dark, claret red flower buds which open to dark orange in mid spring. Foliage dark green with silver underside. Of two-thirds average height and spread. *B.* × *s.* *'Corallina Compacta'* Flower buds bright coral red, yellow on opening. Small foliage, ½in (1cm) long. A very slow dwarf form, rarely exceeding 12-15in (30-40cm) in height and spread. *B.* × *s.* *'Crawley Beauty'* Apricot-yellow flowers in spring; small leaves ½-¾in (1-2cm) long. Makes a low hedge if planted 1½ft (50cm) apart in a single line. A low, slower growing variety reaching 2¼ft (70cm). *B.* × *s.* *'Irwinii'* Flowers deep yellow, borne in profusion along arching stems. Even smaller leaves, narrow, lanceolate, ½in (1cm) long, olive green. When leaves die in autumn, some contrasting red-orange tints seen. Reaching only 2½ft (80cm) in height and 3ft (1m) in width. Slow growth rate. *B.* × *s.* *'Pink Pearl'* An interesting variety of doubtful vigour. The flowers may be creamy-yellow, orange-pink or bi-coloured on different shoots on the same plant. The leaves on new growth are pink or creamy striped in some good seasons; this striping can be very variable. Medium to slow growth rate, reaching 3ft (1m) height and spread.

Average height and spread

Five years
5x5ft (1.5x1.5m)
Ten years
6x6ft (2x2m)
Twenty years
or at maturity
10x10ft (3x3m)

BUDDLEIA DAVIDII

BUTTERFLY BUSH, SUMMER LILAC
Loganiaceae
Deciduous
A beautiful shrub, called Butterfly Bush because of its attraction of butterflies.

Origin From central and western China. Modern forms of garden origin.
Use As large, late summer to early autumn-flowering shrub. Can be trained into small mop-headed tree or fan-trained on a sunless wall.

Buddleia davidii 'Black Knight' in flower

Description *Flower* Fragrant, tubular, pale to mid blue flowers borne in racemes in mid to late summer. Named varieties offer a range of colours from white to almost black. *Foliage* Leaves broad, lanceolate, 4-12in (10-30cm) long, dark to grey-green upper surfaces, light grey to silver undersides; some yellow autumn colour. *Stem* Light to dark green. Strong, upright, becoming slightly spreading, forming a tall shrub. *Fruit* Racemes of light to mid brown seedheads in winter.
Hardiness Tolerates 14°F (−10°C).
Soil Requirements Does best on good, rich, deep soil; tolerates a wide range, both acid and alkaline.
Sun/Shade aspect Full sun to light shade.
Pruning Previous year's wood must be cut back hard in early spring to within 4in (10cm) of its origin. This increases flower size by at least half as much again and extends life of shrub.
Propagation and nursery production From softwood cuttings in summer or hardwood cuttings in winter. Purchase container-grown. Best planting heights 1½-3ft (50cm-1m).
Problems Will be short-lived, with small flowers, unless pruned. May look old and

Buddleia davidii 'Fascinating' in flower

woody when purchased, but grows quickly once planted.

Varieties of interest *B. davidii 'African Queen'* Dark violet flowers, a strong growing variety. *B. d. 'Black Knight'* Dark purple, almost black flowers, with orange eye in centre. Strong to medium growth rate. *B. d. 'Border Beauty'* Crimson red flowers. A lower growing variety, two-thirds average height and spread. *B. d. 'Darkness'* Deep blue to purple-blue flowers. Wide spreading, arching shrub. *B. d. 'Empire Blue'* Violet-blue racemes of tubular flowers with orange eye. Strong, upright stems. *B. d. 'Fascinating'* Extra-large racemes of tubular, lilac-pink flowers. Strong growing. *B. d. 'Fortune'* Long, round racemes of soft lilac flowers with orange eyes. *B. d. 'Harlequin'* Flowers rich purple with broad, lanceolate, creamy white variegated leaves. Two-thirds average height and spread. *B. d. 'Ile de France'* Rich violet flowers. Strong growing. *B. d. 'Nanho Alba'* White flowers,

Buddleia davidii 'Harlequin' in flower

11

Average height and spread

Five years
10x10ft (3x3m)
Ten years
13x13ft (4x4m)
*Twenty years
or at maturity*
13x13ft (4x4m)

slender habit, narrow foliage. Half average height. *B. d. 'Nanho Blue'* Deep blue flowers in short racemes. Half average height with more spreading, graceful, arching, branches. *B. d. 'Nanho Purple'* Purple-blue flowers, low growing. Half average height. *B. d. 'Opera'* Deep purple-red flowers borne on a strong growing shrub. *B. d. 'Orchid Beauty'* Pure mauve flowers. Two-thirds average height. *B. d. 'Peace'* Racemes of white flowers in tubular florets; orange eye in throat. Arching branches. Two-thirds average height. *B. d. 'Purple Prince'* Very large racemes of purple-red flowers. A very strong growing variety with upright branches. *B. d. 'Royal Red'* Rich purple-red racemes of flowers borne on long graceful, arching branches. Two-thirds average height. *B. d. 'Royal Red Variegata'* A white variegated form of the above. *B. d. 'White Bouquet'* Pure white, very fragrant flowers; florets may have yellow eyes. *B. d. 'White Profusion'* Pure white flowers with yellow eyes. Two-thirds average height.

Buddleia davidii
'White Profusion'
in flower

CAMELLIA JAPONICA

KNOWN BY ITS BOTANICAL NAME
Theaceae
Evergreen
Used in the right place, an extremely beautiful plant.

Origin From China and Japan; most varieties now of garden or nursery origin.
Use As an evergreen shrub for acid soils. Very

*Camellia × williamsii
'Donation'* in flower

good for large tubs or containers. Can be fan-trained on a sheltered shady wall to good effect.

Description *Flower* Large, cup-shaped, flowers in a wide range of colours; may be single, semi-double, anemone or peony-shaped, loose double or tight double, depending on variety. Size ranges from small to very large.
Foliage Dark, glossy-green upper surfaces, with grey-green undersides. Ovate to oblong, 3-4in (8-10cm) long and 1½in (4cm) wide.
Stem Bright to dark green, upright, forming a stiff, solid shrub; a few varieties are more laxly presented. Slow to medium growth rate.
Fruit Insignificant.

Hardiness Tolerates 14°F (−10°C), but may shed leaves in harsh conditions, occasionally causing plant to fail.

Soil Requirements Must have acid soil; dislikes any alkalinity.

Sun/Shade aspect Prefers light to mid shade; dislikes full sun.

Pruning None required.May be cut back to keep within bounds. Young plants may be improved by removing one-third of current season's growth, after flowering, for first 2-3 years.

Propagation and nursery production From cuttings in early to mid summer. Purchase container-grown. A limited number of varieties can be found in garden centres; less common varieties must be sought from specialist nurseries. Planting heights 1½-6ft (50cm-2m), ideally 2-2½ft (60-80cm).

Problems Often planted on alkaline soils, where it fails, or in full sun, which it dislikes. Flowers can be damaged by frost in exposed areas.

Varieties of interest *Camellia 'Cornish Snow'* Single, small white flowers; a very attractive small-leaved variety. *C. japonica 'Adolphe Audusson'* Semi-double, blood-red flowers. *C. j. 'Apollo'* Semi-double, rose red flowers, sometimes with white blotches. *C. j. 'Are-*

**Average height
and spread**
Five years
3x3ft (1x1m)
Ten years
6x6ft (2x2m)
*Twenty years
or at maturity*
10x10ft (3x3m)

jishi' Rose red, peony-shaped flowers. *C. j.*
'Betty Sheffield Supreme' Semi-double, white,
peony-shaped flowers with rose pink or red
edges to each petal. *C. j. 'Contessa Lavinia
Maggi'* Double, white or pale pink flowers
with cerise stripes. *C. j. 'Elegans'* Peach pink,
large flowers. Anemone flower formation. *C.
j. 'Madame Victor de Bisschop'* Semi-double,
white flowers. *C. j. 'Mars'* Red, semi-double
flowers. *C. j. 'Mathotiana Alba'* Double,
white flowers of great beauty. *C. j. 'Mathotiana Rosea'* A double pink form. *C. j. 'Mer-
cury'* Deep crimson flowers, semi-double in
form. *C. j. 'Nagasaki'* Semi-double, rose pink
flowers with white stripes. *C. j. 'Tricolor'*
Semi-double white flowers with carmine or
pink stripe. *C. × 'Mary Christian'* Single,
clear pink flowers. Tall-growing. *C. × williamsii 'Donation'* Clear pink, semi-double
flowers. Possibly the best known Camellia.
Height 8ft (2.5m).
The above are just a selected few of the many
hundreds of varieties available.

CHOISYA TERNATA

MEXICAN ORANGE BLOSSOM
Rutaceae
Evergreen
A very attractive, scented, late spring to early summer-flowering
shrub.

Origin From Mexico.
Use As an evergreen shrub for summer
flowering, standing on its own or in a mixed
border. Plant 2½ft (80cm) apart in single line
for an informal hedge.
Description *Flower* Fragrant, single, white,
orange-scented flowers, borne in flat-topped
clusters, late spring to early summer. *Foliage*
Leaves glossy, mid to dark green, trifoliate,
3-6in (8-15cm) long, which when crushed give
off aromatic scent. *Stem* Light to bright green,
glossy, upright, becoming spreading and twiggy with age, forming broad-based, dome-
shaped shrub. Medium growth rate when
young or pruned back, slowing with age. *Fruit*
Insignificant.
Hardiness Tolerates 14°F (−10°C). Leaf damage can occur in lower temperatures or in
severe wind chill. In some winters, may die
back to ground level but can rejuvenate itself
in following spring.
Soil Requirements Does well on most,
although very severe alkaline soils may lead
to chlorosis.
Sun/Shade aspect Equally good in full sun or
deep shade.
Pruning Two methods of pruning are advo-
cated. Cut back to within 1½ft (50cm) of
ground level after 3-4 years, so that it can
rejuvenate itself, and repeat process every
third or fourth year following. This keeps the
foliage glossy and encourages flowering.
Otherwise, on mature shrubs, remove one-
third of the oldest wood to ground level after

**Average height
and spread**
Five years
3x4ft (1x1.2m)
Ten years
6x5½ft (2x1.8m)
*Twenty years
or at maturity*
6x6ft (2x2m)

flowering to encourage rejuvenation from centre and base.

Propagation and nursery production From softwood cuttings taken in summer. Purchase container-grown. Plants are always relatively small when purchased, but quickly mature when planted out. Best planting heights 1-2ft (30-60cm). Availability variable; if not in garden centres and nurseries, must be sought from specialist sources.

Problems If pruning is neglected plant becomes old, woody and unproductive.

Varieties of interest *C. ternata 'Sundance'* Yellow-green in spring, quickly becoming golden yellow which persists through winter. Slightly more tender. Two-thirds average height and spread.

Choisya ternata in flower

CORNUS KOUSA

CHINESE DOGWOOD, JAPANESE DOGWOOD, KOUSA DOGWOOD
Cornaceae
Deciduous
A truly magnificent late spring-flowering shrub with good autumn colour.

Origin From Japan and Korea.
Use As a freestanding shrub for a woodland garden; also well seen when planted with azaleas and rhododendrons. Can be used in a large shrub border but requires space to mature. After 20 or 30 years becomes a small tree.
Description *Flower* Four large creamy white bracts resembling petals, aging to pink-tinged white in late spring, early summer. *Foliage* Leaves elliptic, slightly curled, 2-3in (5-8cm) long, olive green with some purple shading, giving exceptional orange-red autumn colour.

15

Cornus kousa
in flower

Foliage in autumn retained well and is not usually damaged by wind. *Stem* Upright, light green to grey-green, becoming grey-brown and branching with age. Forms upright, slightly spreading shrub in early years, becoming more spreading with age. Slow growth rate at first, then medium, finally becoming less vigorous. *Fruit* Dull red, trawberry-like fruits on mature shrubs.

Hardiness Tolerates 4°F (−15°C).

Soil Requirements Neutral to acid; in moist conditions and light shade, however, may be happy on slightly alkaline soil.

Sun/Shade aspect Prefers light shade; tolerates medium shade to full sun.

Pruning None required.

Propagation and nursery production From layers or softwood cuttings taken in midsum-

Cornus kousa
in autumn

mer. Purchase container-grown. Moderately easy to find. Best planting heights 2-3ft (60cm-1m).

Problems Slow to establish, taking 3-4 years to flower really well.

Varieties of interest *C. capitata* syn. *Benthamia fragifera* Grey-green foliage. Sulphur-yellow bracts, followed in early autumn by strawberry-shaped, orange-red fruits. Winter minimum 23°F (−5°C). *C. kousa chinensis* A Chinese variety which produces larger flowering bracts than its parent. *C. k. 'Gold Spot'* A variety with white flower bracts and with the green foliage mottled with golden variegation. Hard to find. *C. k. 'Milky Way'* An American variety of garden origin with larger white flower bracts. *C. 'Norman Haddon'* Light grey-green foliage with good autumn colour. Pink bracts in late spring. Fruits insignificant. Likely to shed leaves completely in winter.

Average height and spread
Five years
4x3ft (1.2x1m)
Ten years
8x6ft (2.5x2m)
Twenty years or at maturity
12x13ft (3.5x4m)
In favourable conditions can reach 30ft (10m) height and spread.

COTINUS COGGYGRIA

SMOKE TREE, SMOKE BUSH, BURNING BUSH, CHITAM WOOD, VENETIAN SUMACH

Anacardiaceae
Deciduous

A shrub for summer and autumn attraction, producing fine foliage colours, profuse flowers and good structural shape.

Cotinus coggygria 'Foliis Purpureis' in flower

Origin From central and southern Europe.
Use As a foliage shrub for autumn colour and flowers, either on its own or in a large shrub border.
Description *Flower* Large, open, pale pink inflorescences resembling plumes 6-8in (15-20cm) long borne profusely on all wood 3 years old or more in summer, persisting into early and late autumn, turning smoky grey. *Foliage* Leaves ovate to oblong, 1½-2in (4-5cm) long, grey-green when young opening to

17

Cotinus coggygria
'Royal Purple'
in leaf

mid green, vivid orange-yellow in autumn, purple-leaved forms turning scarlet-red. **Stem** Light green, becoming streaked with orange or red shading, finally grey-brown. Fast growing and upright when young, becoming slower and very branching and twiggy to form a round-topped, spreading shrub. **Fruit** Inflorescences change to seedheads.

Hardiness Tolerates 4°F (−15°C). Some winter die-back may occur at tips of new growth.

Soil Requirements Prefers rich, deep soil, but tolerates any.

Sun/Shade aspect Green-leaved varieties tolerate very light shade to full sun. Purple-leaved varieties must have full sun, otherwise they turn green.

Pruning Established plants can be cut to ground level each spring; this produces strong new growth, up to 6ft (2m) in one season with large foliage at the expense of flowers. Or leave completely unpruned to achieve good flowering after 3 or 4 years. Otherwise, it is acceptable to remove mature shoots 1-3 years old each spring, so inducing some foliage rejuvenation and improved flowering.

Propagation and nursery production From layers. Purchase container-grown. Relatively easy to find in nursery production; some varieties will be found in garden centres. Best planting heights 15in-2½ft (40-80cm).

Problems Some purple-leaved varieties susceptible to mildew. Slow to establish, taking 2-3 years after planting to gain full stature.

Varieties of interest *C. c. 'Flame'* One of the best varieties for autumn colour. Pink flowers and bright red-orange foliage in autumn. Hard to find and often confused with *C. coggygria* itself. *C. c. 'Foliis Purpureis'* Pink inflorescence, young foliage rich plum-purple, aging to lighter red to purple-red, late summer. Good autumn colours. *C. c. 'Notcutt's Variety'* Pink to purple-pink inflorescence with good red-purple autumn colours. Very deep purple leaves, slightly larger than

Average height and spread
Five years
5x5½ft (1.5x1.8m)
Ten years
10x10ft (3x3m)
Twenty years or at maturity
20x20ft (6x6m)

those of its parent. Of slightly less height and spread. ***C. c. 'Royal Purple'*** Purple-pink inflorescence, purple-wine foliage, almost translucent when seen with sunlight behind it, becoming duller purple towards autumn, finally red. Slightly smaller than *C. coggygria*. Of garden origin. ***C. c. 'Rubrifolius'*** Pink inflorescence, deep wine red leaves when young, translucent in sunlight, becoming red-green towards autumn. Good autumn colours. ***C. obovatus*** syn. ***C. o. americanus*** (Chitam Wood) Light pink inflorescence. Round, ovate, light to mid green foliage with some orange shading, brilliant orange-red in autumn. Leaves much larger than *C. coggygria*. Forming a large, spreading shrub. From south-eastern USA.

Cotinus obovatus
in flower

CRATAEGUS OXYACANTHA

THORN, MAY, HAWTHORN
Rosaceae
Deciduous
With other cut-leaved species and varieties listed, a group of attractive and reliable trees for late spring flowering.

Origin From Europe.
Use Ideal small round-topped trees for all types of garden. Can be severely pruned to control or shape the growth. Also useful for street planting due to the neat, tight, compact habit.
Description *Flower* Clusters of white, pink or red flowers, single or double depending on variety. Flower clusters up to 2in (5cm) across, produced in late spring. Musty scent attractive to bees. *Foliage* Basically ovate, 2in (5cm) long, very deeply lobed with 3 or 5 indentations. Grey-green with some yellow

Crataegus oxyacantha 'Paul's Scarlet' in flower

autumn tints. **Stem** Light grey-green, becoming grey-brown. Strong, upright when young, quickly branching. Armed with small, extremely sharp spines up to ½in (1cm) long. Medium rate of growth, forming a round-topped tree which spreads with age. **Fruit** Small, dull red, round to oval fruits produced in autumn containing two stone seeds, a distinctive characteristic.

Hardiness Tolerant of −13°F (−25°C).

Soil Requirements Any soil conditions, but shows signs of distress on extremely dry areas, where growth may be stunted.

Sun/Shade aspect Tolerates full sun to medium shade, preferring light shade.

Pruning None required, but responds well to being cut back hard if necessary.

Propagation and nursery production From seed for the parent; all varieties budded or grafted. Plant bare-rooted or container-grown. Available from 3ft (1m) up to 13ft (4m). Best planting heights 5½-6ft (1.8-2m).

Problems The sharp spines can make cultivation difficult. Suckers of understock may appear and must be removed.

Varieties of interest *C. laciniata* syn. *C. orientalis* Attractive dark grey-green, cut-leaved foliage, light grey undersides. White flowers and large dull orange-red fruits. Two-thirds average height and spread. Somewhat scarce in production. From the Orient. *C. monogyna* (Hedgerow Thorn, Singleseed Hawthorn) Single white flowers. Red, round fruits containing one stone. Foliage dark green. Rarely offered as a tree, normally used as a hedgerow plant. From Europe. *C. 'Stricta'* White flowers followed by orange-red berries. Upright growth of average height, maximum spread of 4ft (1.2m). Useful as a street tree or for planting in confined spaces. *C. × mordenensis 'Toba'* Double, creamy white flowers in the spring, followed by red berries in autumn. *C. oxyacantha 'Alba Plena'* Double white flowers in mid spring, followed by limited numbers of·

Average height and spread

Five years
13x4ft (4x1.2m)
Ten years
20x10ft (6x3m)
Twenty years or at maturity
20x20ft (6x6m)

red berries in autumn. *C. o. 'Crimson Cloud'* Profuse single, dark pink to red flowers with yellow eyes in late spring. Good yellow-bronze-orange autumn colour. *C. o. 'Fastigiata'* Single white flowers, limited red berries. A narrow, columnar tree of average height and no more than 6ft (2m) spread. *C. o. 'Gireoudii'* New foliage on new growth mottled pink and white, aging to green. New foliage on old wood green. Bush-forming. Two-thirds average height and spread. A light annual pruning of outer extremities in early spring is recommended to encourage new variegated growth. Shy to flower, but can produce white, musty-scented flowers. Limited fruit production. Difficult to find and must be sought from specialist nurseries. *C. o. 'Paul's Scarlet'* syn. *C. o. 'Coccinea Plena'* Dark pink to red, double flowers produced late spring, early summer. Limited red berries in autumn. *C. o. 'Rosea Plena'* Double pink flowers. Produced late spring, early summer. Some limited berrying.

Crataegus oxyacantha **'Rosea Plena'** **in flower**

CYTISUS × PRAECOX

WARMINSTER BROOM

Leguminosae
Deciduous
Beautiful spring-flowering shrubs worthy of any garden.

Origin Of garden origin. Originally found in Wiltshire, England.
Use In shrub borders as a useful, low to medium height shrub for single or mass planting. Good in tubs of adequate size. Sometimes supplied grafted on to 4ft (1.2m) high stem of *Laburnum vulgaris* to make small to medium height weeping standard.
Description *Flower* Small pea-flowers, white,

cream, yellow, pink or red, according to variety, freely borne, late spring. *Foliage* Leaves lanceolate, grey-green, ½-¾in (1-2cm) long, sparsely produced, chiefly towards base of branches. *Stem* Grey-green to light green, upright when young, becoming arching to form a very attractive shape. Medium to fast growth rate. *Fruit* Insignificant.

Hardiness Tolerates 14°F (−10°C).

Soil Requirements Does well on most soils but extreme alkalinity may lead to severe chlorosis.

Sun/Shade aspect Full sun.

Pruning None required, but small sections of year-old growth may be removed after flowering.

Propagation and nursery production From softwood cuttings taken in early summer. Purchase container-grown. *C. × praecox* and *C. × p. 'Allgold'* are fairly easy to find, but other varieties less common. Best planting heights 15in-2ft (40-60cm).

Problems Rather short-lived and should be replaced after 10-15 years. Has a poor root system and mature plants may need staking in exposed areas.

Varieties of interest *C. × p. 'Albus'* Pure white flowers. Vigorous and of slightly more height and spread than average. *C. × p. 'Allgold'*

Cytisus × praecox 'Albus' in flower

Average height and spread

Five years
2½x3ft (80cmx1m)
Ten years
3x5ft (1x1.5m)
Twenty years or at maturity
4x6ft (1.2x2m)

Golden yellow flowers. *C. × p. 'Buttercup'* Buttercup yellow flowers. *C. 'Hollandia'* Purple-red flowers. *C. 'Zeelandia'* Pink and mauve bicoloured flowers. One-third more than average height and spread.

CYTISUS SCOPARIUS

BROOM
Leguminosae
Deciduous
Very attractive spring-flowering shrubs, but relatively short-lived.

Origin Basic form from Europe, but mostly of garden origin.
Use As freestanding flowering shrubs for larger shrub borders, or for single or mass planting.

Cystisus scoparius 'Andreanus' **in flower**

Description *Flower* Scented pea-flowers, pink, red, amber, yellow, bronze, or bicoloured, late spring, early summer. *Foliage* Leaves sparsely produced, small, lanceolate, ½-¾in (1-2cm) long, grey-green, borne chiefly on low branches. *Stem* Long, angular, upright, becoming spreading; light green to grey-green. Fast-growing when young, slowing with age. *Fruit* Small, grey-green pods may be produced in winter.
Hardiness Tolerates 14°F (−10°C).
Soil Requirements Prefers neutral to acid soil, dislikes alkalinity but tolerates it provided depth of topsoil is adequate.
Sun/Shade aspect Best in full sun.
Pruning Best unpruned so as to reach full size, but if desired current season's growth can be halved after flowering. Cutting into older wood may lead to total die-back.
Propagation and nursery production From softwood cuttings taken in early summer. Purchase container-grown. Limited range of varieties at nurseries and garden centres; some varieties may have to be sought from specialist sources. Best planting heights 2-2½ft (60-80cm).
Problems Brooms are all relatively short-lived and after 10-12 years should be replaced. Varieties of *C. scoparius* root poorly; taller plants may need staking.

Cytisus scoparius
'Cornish Cream'
in flower

**Average height
and spread**
Five years
6x5ft (2x1.5m)
Ten years
10x6ft (3x2m)
*Twenty years
or at maturity*
10x8ft (3x2.5m)

Varieties of interest *C. nigricans* Yellow pea-flowers produced in terminal racemes in mid to late summer. Of slightly more than average height and spread. Scarce in production. From central and south-eastern Europe through to central Russia. *C. scoparius* *'Andreanus'* Bicoloured, crimson-red and chrome yellow flowers. *C. s. 'Cornish Cream'* Bicoloured cream-yellow flowers borne on strong, upright branches. *C. s. 'Fulgens'* Bicoloured amber and rich crimson flowers carried on stiff, strong branches. *C. s. 'Red Favourite'* Deep red flowers, upright stems. **Hybrids:** *C. 'Burkwoodii'* Maroon and bright red flowers. Upright when young, becoming arching with age. *C. 'C.E. Pearson'* Rose pink, yellow and red flowers. *C. 'Criterion'* Bicoloured, brown-purple flowers. Strong-growing. Slightly more than average height and spread. *C. 'Daisy Hill'* Bicoloured crimson and cream flowers, graceful arching stems. Above average spread. *C. 'Donard*

Cytisus 'Killiney
Salmon' in flower

24

Seedling' Bicoloured mauve, red and pink flowers on strong, stout branches. Above average height and spread. *C. 'Dorothy Walpole'* Bicoloured crimson-pink flowers. Strong growth. *C. 'Eastern Queen'* Bicoloured amber and crimson flowers. Strong growth. *C. 'Golden Cascade'* Large, golden yellow flowers. Arched, weeping stems. *C. 'Goldfinch'* Golden yellow flowers. Upright. One-third less than average height and spread. *C. 'Killiney Salmon'* Red-salmon flowers. Graceful habit. Slightly more than average height and spread. *C. 'Lord Lambourne'* Bicoloured cream and maroon flowers. *C. 'Minstead'* Flowers white flushed lilac with darker outer wings. Thin stems and graceful, lax habit. One-third more than average height and spread. *C. 'Moonlight'* Delicate sulphur yellow flowers. *C. 'Windlesham Ruby'* Mahogany-crimson flowers. Arching branches.

DAPHNE MEZEREUM

FEBRUARY DAPHNE, MEZEREON

Thymelaeaceae
Deciduous
A very popular, attractive scented shrub, flowering winter to early spring.

Origin From Europe, including British Isles, through Asia Minor and Siberia.
Use As a low, winter-flowering shrub for borders, large rock gardens or the edges of a shrub border.

Daphne mezereum
'Alba' in flower

Description *Flower* Small, purple-red, or white, dependent on variety, scented, trumpet-shaped flowers borne thickly along the entire length of upright shoots, late winter to early spring. *Foliage* Leaves small, round-ended, lanceolate, 1½-2in (4-5cm) long, grey-green with some yellow autum colour.

25

Stem Light grey to grey-green, upright and of rubbery texture, forming a goblet-shaped shrub. Slow to medium growth rate. **Fruit** Round, yellow aging to red, poisonous fruits borne more or less freely, depending on dryness of season. Seed often germinates into young plants at base of parent plant.

Hardiness Tolerates 14°F (−10°C).

Soil Requirements Prefers rich, deep, leafy loam; tolerates moderately high alkalinity but dislikes waterlogging.

Sun/Shade aspect Prefers light shade, tolerates full sun.

Pruning None required.

Propagation and nursery production From seed or layers. Plants produced from layers from a known parent can have better flower production. Purchase container-grown or root-balled (balled-and-burlapped). Normally available when in flower from both nurseries and garden centres. Best planting heights 15in-2½ft (40-80cm).

Problems Genetic virus can lead to sudden death of mature specimens, as with most Daphnes. The virus can cause the foliage to look diseased, though without affecting flowering or fruiting.

Daphne mezereum in flower

Average height and spread

Five years
2x1½ft (60x50cm)
Ten years
2½x2¼ft (80x70cm)
*Twenty years
or at maturity*
2½x3ft (80cmx1m)

Varieties of interest *D. bholua* Flowers red-mauve in bud, opening to white with red-mauve reverses to each petal. Sweetly scented and borne in terminal clusters in midwinter. Extremely scarce in production. *D. genkwa* Fragrant lilac-blue flowers produced on branches which are leafless in early spring. From China and Taiwan. Extremely difficult to find; must be sought from specialist nurseries. *D. mezereum 'Alba'* White to green-white scented flowers, late winter to early spring. A slightly less vigorous form and more difficult to find. *D. m. 'Alba Bowle's Hybrid'* A hybrid propagated from layers, producing slightly larger green-white flowers than *D. m. 'Alba'*. Stock always small when supplied, and usually with single stem. *D. m. 'Grandiflora'* Larger flowers, rich purple, often appearing mid to late autumn. Very scarce. *D. m. 'Rubrum'* A European variety with very good large, purple-red flowers.

DEUTZIA

KNOWN BY BOTANICAL NAME
Philadelphaceae
Deciduous
A range of very free-flowering early summer shrubs of widely varying sizes and shapes.

Origin Mainly from China, but many varieties of garden or nursery origin.

Use For shrub borders or group plantings, or as a freestanding specimen.

Description *Flower* Small, short panicles of bell-shaped flowers in shades of white or pink through to purple-pink, depending on variety; late spring to early summer. *Foliage* Leaves small to medium, ovate, 1½-4in (4-10cm) long, olive green, giving some yellow or purple autumn colour depending on variety. *Stem* Mostly upright, strong, light grey to grey-green, becoming very twiggy and branching with age; some varieties more arching and pendulous. Medium growth rate. *Fruit* Grey-brown seedheads in autumn, retained into winter.

Hardiness Tolerates −13°F (−25°C).

Soil Requirements Prefers moist, good soil, tolerates high alkalinity. If grown on dry soils must be watered, particularly during droughts.

Sun/Shade aspect Full sun to light shade.

Pruning Remove one-third of oldest flowering wood after flowering.

Propagation and nursery production From semi-ripe cuttings taken midsummer or from hardwood cuttings taken late autumn and winter. Purchase container-grown or bare-rooted. Most varieties fairly easy to find. Best planting heights 2-2½ft (60-80cm).

Problems May not survive drought.

Varieties of interest *D. chunii* Single flowers, pink outside, white within, with yellow

Deutzia gracilis
in flower

27

Deutzia × kalmiiflora
in flower

anthers, produced in 2in (5cm) panicles. Very scarce. **D. 'Contraste'** Panicles of star-shaped, semi-double flowers, soft lilac-pink on outer side, rich purple inner side. Reaches one-third average height and spread. An outstanding variety. Of garden origin. **D. corymbosa** Open, short racemes of single white flowers in early summer. Half average height and spread. Best planting heights 15in-2ft (40-60cm). **D. × elegantissima** Rose pink, fragrant paniculated clusters of flowers, early to mid summer. Half average height and spread with much thinner, more twiggy growth. **D. × elegantissima 'Rosealind'** Single, deep carmine-pink flowers in short panicles, borne freely on thin, wispy, arching branches, early summer. Half average height and spread. Best planting heights 15in-1½ft (40-50cm). **D. gracilis** (Slender Deutzia, Japanese Snow Flower) Pure white single flowers. From Japan. **D. × kalmiiflora** Very short

Deutzia 'Mont Rose'
in flower

racemes or singly produced flowers, pink to flushed carmine, borne on arching branches, late spring. Good plum-purple autumn colours. One-third average height and spread. Of garden origin. Best planting heights 15in-2ft (40-60cm). *D. longifolia 'Veitchii'* Clusters of single, lilac-pink flowers, early summer. Foliage long, more lanceolate and lighter green than most Deutzias. Of garden origin. *D. 'Magicien'* Large, mauve-pink, single flowers with white edges and purple reverses. Of garden origin. *D.* × *magnifica* Double pure white flowers, early summer. A strong-growing variety. Of garden origin. *D. monbeigii* Single, white, star-like flowers profusely produced in late summer. Smaller leaves with white undersides and slightly arching branches. One-third average height and spread. From China. *D. 'Mont Rose'* Single to semi-double, rose pink flowers with darker highlights, produced in large paniculated clusters, early summer. Of garden origin. *D. pulchra* Racemes of pure white flowers in long, hanging, lily-of-the-valley type formation. Two-thirds average height and spread and very hardy. From Taiwan. *D.* × *rosea 'Carminea'* Flowers rose-carmine with paler shading. Two-thirds average height and spread. Of garden origin. *D. scabra* (Fuzzy Deutzia) Single white flowers in panicle-shaped clusters, early summer. Very upright habit. From Japan. *D. s. 'Candidissima'* Pure white, double flowers, early summer. Upright. Of garden origin. *D. s. 'Plena'* Double, rose purple flowers with white shading. Of garden origin. *D. s. 'Pride of Rochester'* Double white flowers produced in early summer. Upright. Of garden origin. *D. setchuenensis* Clusters of small white, star-like flowers profusely borne, mid to late summer. Two-thirds average height and spread. Slightly less hardy. From China.

Average height and spread
Five years
6x3ft (2x1m)
Ten years
10x6ft (3x2m)
Twenty years or at maturity
13x10ft (4x3m)

ESCALLONIA

KNOWN BY BOTANICAL NAME
Escalloniaceae
Evergreen
Handsome early summer-flowering shrubs with an attractive range of flower colours.

Origin From South America. Nearly all varieties offered are of garden or nursery origin.
Use As a freestanding evergreen or for large shrub borders. If planted 2½ft (80cm) apart in single row makes good semi-formal evergreen hedge.
Description *Flower* Single or in short racemes, bell-shaped flowers, various shades of pink to pink-red; some white forms. Late spring through to early summer, with intermittent flowering through late summer and early autumn. *Foliage* Leaves ovate, 1-1½in (3-4cm) long, with indented edges. Light to dark green glossy upper surfaces, grey undersides. Size of foliage varies according to variety.

Escallonia 'Crimson Spire' in flower

Stem Upright when young, becoming arching according to variety, and branching with age. Grey-green. Fast growth rate when young, slowing with age. **Fruit** Insignificant.

Hardiness Tolerates 14°F (−10°C).

Soil Requirements Tolerates most soils but liable to chlorosis on extremely alkaline types.

Sun/Shade aspect Full sun through to medium shade.

Pruning Remove one-third of old flowering wood after main flowering period. If cut to ground level will rejuvenate after second or third spring.

Propagation and nursery production From softwood cuttings taken midsummer. Purchase container-grown. Most varieties fairly

Escallonia 'Donard Seedling' in flower

easy to find. Best planting heights 2-2½ft (60-80cm).

Problems Susceptible to severe wind chill and may lose leaves completely. Normally rejuvenates from ground level, but may take 2-3 years to reach previous height.

Varieties of interest *E. 'Apple Blossom'* Flowers apple blossom pink, large and normally borne singly. Slightly upright. *E. 'C.F. Ball'* Rich red flowers and medium-sized foliage. Slightly arching. *E. 'Crimson Spire'* Crimson flowers and medium-sized foliage. Upright, good for hedging. Slightly less than average spread. *E. 'Donard Beauty'* Large rose carmine flowers and large green foliage. Slightly arching. Takes its name from the Slieve Donard Nurseries in Northern Ireland, where several of the varieties listed below were raised. *E. 'Donard Brilliance'* Large rose red

Escallonia 'Iveyi'
in flower

flowers and large foliage. Upright, becoming spreading with age. *E. 'Donard Gem'* Pale pink flowers, slightly scented. *E. 'Donard Radiance'* Medium-sized, rich pink flowers and large foliage. Slightly arching. *E. 'Donard Seedling'* Medium-sized flowers, pink in bud, opening to white tinted with rose. Large leaves. Slightly arching. *E. 'Donard Star'* Large deep rosy pink flowers. Large foliage. Upright, becoming spreading. *E. 'Edinensis'* Medium-sized, carmine-pink flowers. Large foliage. Arching. *E. 'Gwendolyn Anley'* Small flowers, pink in bud, opening to paler pink. Small foliage. Arching, spreading and very twiggy. Two-thirds average height and spread. Best planting heights 12-15in (30-40cm). *E. 'Ingramii'* Rose pink flowers, medium size. Large foliage. Arching. Height and spread 6ft (2m). *E. 'Iveyi'* Large pure white flowers. Large dark green, shiny foliage. Upright, becoming slightly spreading with age. *E. 'Langleyensis'* Small, bright carmine-rose flowers in profusion along arching branches. Small leaved. *E. macrantha*

**Average height
and spread**
Five years
6x6ft (2x2m)
Ten years
10x13ft (3x4m)
*Twenty years
or at maturity*
10x13ft (3x4m)

31

Medium-sized rose carmine flowers, large, scented, dark green foliage. Upright and branching. Good in coastal areas. Less than average hardiness. Height and spread slightly larger than average in favourable areas. *E. 'Peach Blossom'* Good-sized clear pink flowers. Large foliage. Arching. *E. rubra 'Woodside'* syn. *'Pygmaea'* Small, dark pink to red flowers. Small cut foliage, light green, not glossy. Height 1½ft (50cm), spread 2ft (80cm). Best planting heights 12-15in (30-40cm). *E. 'Slieve Donard'* Small pale pink flowers in profusion, borne on long, arching branches. Slightly less than average height and spread.

HYDRANGEA MACROPHYLLA
Hortensia varieties

BIGLEAF HYDRANGEA, MOP-HEADED HYDRANGEA
Hydrangeaceae
Deciduous
One of the more spectacular summer-flowering shrubs, worthy of any garden, although there is some colour variation and a fairly precise planting position is required.

Origin Basic forms from Japan; most varieties now offered are of garden or nursery origin.
Use As a freestanding, flowering shrub, either singly, massed or in groups. Can be used in large containers not less than 2½ft (80cm) across and 2ft (60cm) deep but must be given adequate in-season feeding.
Description *Flower* Large, round, sterile heads, ranging through white, pink, red, blue or combinations of these, aging to darker, more metallic shades from midsummer to well into winter, when flowers turn bronze-

Hydrangea macrophylla 'Generale Vicomtesse de Vibraye' in flower

brown. Exact shade depends both on variety and on soil in which it is grown. Many forms on acid soil will be blue, on neutral soil red and on alkaline soil pink. Plants may be shy to flower unless planted as indicated by soil, sun and shade requirements. *Foliage* Leaves ovate, 4-8in (10-20cm) long and 6-8in (15-20cm) wide, light to mid green, sometimes dark green on rich moist soil. Yellow autumn colouring. *Stem* Creamy brown mature stems, upright, branching and forming a round, tall, mound-shaped shrub. Medium to fast growth rate. *Fruit* None.

Hydrangea macrophylla 'Miss Belgium' in flower

Hardiness Tolerates 4°F (−15°C), although late spring frosts may damage new foliage.
Soil Requirements Deep, moist soil. Any drying out will be shown by poor growth and flagging foliage. Water freely in time of drought.
Sun/Shade aspect Light shade. Dislikes both full sun and deep shade, which spoils shape and reduces flowering.
Pruning None required. Oversized shrubs may be cut to ground level, but will take 3-4 seasons to come back to full flowering. On mature plants thin one-third of weakest growth annually, in very cold areas not before early spring.
Propagation and nursery production From softwood cuttings. Purchase container-grown. Most common forms fairly easy to find in garden centres but some forms may need searching for in specialist nurseries. Best planting heights 1½-2½ft (50-80cm).
Problems Light shade and good, rich, moist soil are essential requirements for good flowering.
Varieties of interest Because the flower colour varies according to alkaline or acid conditions, the first colour given below is that for alkaline soil, the second that which can be expected on acid soil. *H. m. 'Altona'* Cherry pink or mid blue. *H. m. 'Ami Pasquier'*

Average height and spread
Five years
3x3ft (1x1m)
Ten years
6x6ft (2x2m)
Twenty years or at maturity
10x10ft (3x3m)

Crimson or purple-red. *H. m. 'Amethyst'* Pink or purple. *H. m. 'Ayesha'* Pink or grey-lilac. *H. m. 'Blue Prince'* Rose red or cornflower blue. *H. m. 'Deutschland'* Pale pink or pink-blue. *H. m. 'Europa'* Pale pink-blue or clear blue. *H. m. 'Generale Vicomtesse de Vibraye'* Pink or clear blue. *H. m. 'Hamburg'* Pink-rose or purple-rose. *H. m. 'Harry's Red'* Red or deep red. *H. m. 'Holstein'* Pink or sky blue. *H. m. 'King George'* Pale pink or dark, rich, rose pink. *H. m. 'Klus Supreme'* Deep pink or dark blue. *H. m. 'Madame Emile Mouillière'* White with some pink shading or pure white. *H. m. 'Maréchal Foch'* Deep pink or deep blue. *H. m. 'Miss Belgium'* Red to rose red. *H. m. 'Niedersachsen'* Pale pink or pale blue. *H. m. 'President Doumer'* Purple-red or blue. *H. m. 'Sister Teresa'* Pure white on both soil types.

HYDRANGEA MACROPHYLLA
Lacecap varieties

LACECAP HYDRANGEA
Hydrangeaceae
Deciduous
Given the right soil conditions and required shade, these later summer-flowering shrubs provide a most effective display.

Origin From Japan, but most varieties of garden or nursery origin.
Use As an individual shrub, for mass planting, good for shady areas. Or for planting in tubs not less than 2½ft (80cm) across and 2ft (60cm) deep. Use good potting medium and feed adequately in season. Can be forced for the purpose of making a houseplant and planted out after flowering.
Description *Flower* Round central clusters of flowers, white, through pink to blue surrounded by bold ray florets, late summer and

Hydrangea macrophylla 'Blue Wave' in flower

early autumn. *Foliage* Leaves large, ovate, 4-8in (10-20cm) long and 4-6in (10-15cm) wide, light to mid green, giving some plum autumn colour. *Stem* Upright when young, becoming spreading with age, forming a wide, spreading, dome-shaped shrub. Grey to creamy brown. Medium to fast growth rate. *Fruit* None. Dead brown flowerheads may be maintained well into autumn.

Hardiness Tolerates 4°F (−15°C); late spring frosts may damage newly opened foliage, but this readily rejuvenates.

Hydrangea macrophylla 'White Wave' in flower

Soil Requirements Prefers rich, deep acid soil; tolerates wide range but dislikes very dry soils. Blue flower colour is turned pink by alkaline soils. White varieties maintain colour on both types of soil.

Sun/Shade aspect Light shade. Dislikes both full sun and deep shade. Lack of light spoils shape and dryness leads to very poor results.

Pruning Thin lightly, removing older, weaker shoots each winter, or in spring in colder areas. Avoid cutting back hard as this stops the following year's flowering.

Propagation and nursery production From cuttings. Purchase container-grown. All varieties fairly easy to find, especially when in flower. Best planting heights 1½-2½ft (50-80cm).

Problems Requirements of light shade and good, rich, moist soil must be met for full flowering.

Varieties of interest *H. m. 'Blue Wave'* Central, fertile, tufted flowers with numerous outer, large ray florets. Pink on alkaline soils, blue on acid, almost gentian blue in very acid conditions. *H. m. 'Lanarth White'* Central fertile flowers pink on alkaline soils, blue on acid, with outer ray florets pure white. Slightly more compact than most. *H. m. 'Lilacina'* Central flowers amethyst blue with pink ray florets on alkaline or blue on acid soils. May be difficult to find. *H. m. 'Maculata'* syn. *H. m. 'Variegata'* Flowers white to pink-white in

Average height and spread
Five years
3x4ft (1x1.2m)
Ten years
5½x6ft (1.8x2m)
Twenty years or at maturity
5½x12ft (1.8x3.5m)

colour. May be blue-white on acid soils. Leaves green to grey-green with creamy white margins. *H. m. 'Mariesii'* Central fertile flowers rosy pink to blue-pink on acid soils, with outer ray florets varying shades of blue, or pink on alkaline soil. *H. m. 'Sea Foam'* Blue, fertile central flowers surrounded by white ray florets. Very good in coastal areas but not fully hardy inland. Not always easy to find. *H. m. 'Tricolor'* Flowers pale pink on alkaline soil or pure white on acid, slightly smaller than those of most varieties and less reliably produced. Good, mid green foliage with grey or pale yellow outer variegation. *H. m. 'Veitchii'* Central fertile flowers pink on alkaline soils and blue on acid, having outer white florets which fade to pink. One of the hardiest varieties. *H. m. 'White Wave'* syn. *H. m. 'Mariesii Alba'*, *H. m. 'Mariesii Grandiflora'* Central fertile flowers pink to lilac-blue on acid soils, large white outer ray florets. Dark green, large, healthy foliage. A very good growing form.

KOLKWITZIA AMABILIS

BEAUTY BUSH
Caprifoliaceae
Deciduous
An often overlooked shrub for late spring to early summer flowering, but a real beauty, as its common name implies.

Origin From western China.
Use As a medium-sized to large shrub to stand on its own forming an attractive symmetrical clump or for a shrub border. Can be used as an informal hedge planted 3ft (1m) apart.
Description *Flower* Bell-shaped, soft pink with yellow throat, hanging in small clusters along wood 3 years old, late spring, early summer and midsummer. *Foliage* Leaves medium to small, ovate, 1-1½in (3-4cm) long, slightly tooth-edged, light olive green to grey-green with red shading and silver undersides. Yellow autumn colour. *Stem* Young shoots light green to green-brown. Strong and upright being produced mainly from ground level. Growth more than 2 years old becomes slightly arched, spreading and twiggy. Fast to medium growth rate. *Fruit* Small, grey-brown, slightly translucent seeds.
Hardiness Tolerates low winter temperatures in the range 4°F (−15°C) down to −13°F (−25°C).
Soil Requirements Any soil, no preferences.
Sun/Shade aspect Prefers full sun, tolerates light shade.
Pruning Remove one-third of oldest flowering wood by cutting to ground level after the flowering period.
Propagation and nursery production From soft to semi-ripe cuttings taken midsummer, or from hardwood cuttings taken in winter. Plant bare-rooted or container-grown. Best planting heights 1½-2½ft (50-80cm).
Problems When purchased container-grown presents very fragile, weak appearance but

Average height and spread
Five years
5x5ft (1.5x1.5m)
Ten years
8x8ft (2.5x2.5m)
Twenty years or at maturity
10x10ft (3x3m)

Kolkwitzia amabilis
in flower

rapidly becomes robust once planted out.
Varieties of interest *K. a. 'Pink Cloud'* A
cultivar of garden origin, with large, strong
pink flowers, possibly better for garden planting than the parent.

LABURNUM ALPINUM

ALPINE LABURNUM, SCOTCH LABURNUM
Leguminosae
Deciduous
Sometimes overlooked, but a very attractive tree, especially the
dark green foliage. The weeping form can be used to great
advantage as a specimen or feature plant in the smallest of
gardens.

Origin From central and southern Europe.
Use As a small ornamental tree, flowering in
late spring or early summer when many other
flowering trees have finished. Also used as a
bush or as a standard tree, and in its weeping
form for tubs and containers.
Description *Flower* Pendulous racemes of
fragrant, golden yellow flowers in late spring
or early summer. *Foliage* Olive green, trifoli-

Laburnum alpinum
'Pendulum' in flower

37

**Average height
and spread**
Five years
13x6ft (4x2m)
Ten years
13x10ft (4x3m)
*Twenty years
or at maturity*
23x13ft (7x4m)

ate leaves, glossy upper surfaces and paler slightly hairy undersides. *Stem* Olive green upright stems when young. Spreading with age to form a dome-shaped large bush or standard tree. *Fruit* Poisonous, hanging, grey-green, small, pea-pod type fruits, often in great profusion, especially on mature plants.
Hardiness Tolerates −13°F (−25°C).
Soil Requirements Most soil types; likes very alkaline forms. Extremely wet conditions may lead to root-damage and unstable anchorage. Tub-grown plants need a large container and good potting soil.
Sun/Shade aspect Best in full sun, but tolerates quite deep shade.
Pruning None required; may even resent it.
Propagation and nursery production *L. alpinum* grown from seed; 'Pendulum' form is grafted. Can be purchased bare-rooted or container-grown.
Problems Susceptible to blackfly (aphid), a winter host to this pest. Poisonous pods are dangerous to children.
Varieties of interest *L. a. 'Pendulum'* A good weeping form, reaching only about 10ft (3m) in height unless grafted. Slow-growing and weeping to the ground, with a spread of 5ft (1.5m) in time. Good display of hanging yellow flowers late spring, early summer. Grafts on a 5ft (1.5m) or 8ft (2.5m) stem can look unsightly in early years.

LAVANDULA

LAVENDER
Labiatae
Evergreen
Lavenders are among the most useful of all summer-flowering low shrubs, with the bonus of the very pleasant lavender scent.

Origin From Europe.
Use As low shrubs for edging in shrub borders, planted singly or in groups. Dwarf varieties are useful for underplanting, for example in rose beds. Larger types may be planted 15in (40cm) apart in a single line to make a low informal hedge.
Description *Flower* Borne in upright spikes, produced above foliage, in varying shades of blue, pink or white, depending on variety, mid to late summer. Very sweetly scented with typical lavender perfume. Attractive and fragrant when dried. *Foliage* Sparsely produced, narrow, lanceolate, ½-1in (2-3cm) long, grey-green to silver-green. *Stem* Short, limited branching, upright stems, surmounted by tall, bare, flowering stems. Grey to silver-grey. Fast growth rate, slowing with age. *Fruit* Large seedheads retained into winter.
Hardiness Tolerates 14°F (−10°C).
Soil Requirements Light, well-drained soil; dislikes waterlogging.
Sun/Shade aspect Full sun, dislikes any shade.
Pruning A light to medium trimming each

spring, just as new growth starts, encourages rejuvenation of new foliage and increases the number of flower spikes. In addition, the removal of dying flower spikes is advised. Old plants can be cut back hard in spring, and will normally rejuvenate.

Propagation and nursery production From semi-ripe cuttings taken in early summer. Purchase container-grown or bare-rooted. Some forms easy to find, although specific varieties may have to be sought from specialist sources. Best planting heights 4-15in (10-40cm).

Problems Young plants when purchased in late spring or early summer look very good, but as autumn approaches can become old and woody; however once planted they quickly produce new growth in following spring.

Varieties of interest *L. angustifolia* syn. *L. officinalis*, *L. spica* (Old English Lavender) Mid blue flower spikes, produced on long slender stems, good silver-grey foliage. *L. a. 'Alba'* A white form of Old English Lavender. Off-white flowers on long stems, produced mid to late summer. Rather hard to find. *L. a. 'Folgate'* Lavender-blue flowers, late summer, narrow, silvery grey-green leaves. A good, compact form. *L. a. 'Grappenhall'* Lavender-blue flowers in midsummer, grey-green leaves. *L. a. 'Hidcote'* Violet-blue, very thick spikes of scented flowers in midsummer, surmounting grey-green foliage. Possibly one of the best varieties, good for hedging or underplanting. Compact in growth, rarely reaching more than 1½ft (50cm) in height and spread. *L. a. 'Loddon Pink'* Blue to pink-blue spikes of flowers on long stems in midsummer, surmounting grey-green foliage. *L. a. 'Munstead'* Lavender-blue flowers in midsummer. Good for hedging or underplanting. Height 1½ft (50cm). *L. a. 'Nana Alba'* A white form, reaching no more than 1ft (30cm)

Lavandula angustifolia 'Hidcote' **in flower**

Average height and spread
Five years
1½x2ft (50x60cm)
Ten years
2½x2½ft (80x80cm)
Twenty years or at maturity
3x3ft (1x1m)

in height. Scarce and hard to find. *L. a.* *'Rosea'* Blue-pink to pink flowers, in midsummer. A good, compact plant. *L. a.* *'Twicket Purple'* Lavender-blue to purple flowers, in midsummer. A tight-growing form with grey-green foliage. *L. a. 'Vera'* (Dutch Lavender) Lavender-blue flowers in midsummer. Foliage grey-green and broader than most. Good, strong-growing variety, slightly more than average height and spread.

MAGNOLIA
Large-growing, star-flowered varieties

STAR MAGNOLIA
Magnoliaceae
Deciduous
Large, early spring-flowering shrubs for very attractive featured flower display.

Origin From Japan.
Use As a large freestanding shrub, or small tree. A good feature at the back of a large shrub border if adequate space is available.
Description *Flower* Multi-petalled, star-shaped, white or pink, dependent on variety, fragrant flowers produced in numbers up to 15-20 years after planting, after which flowering increases to give glorious display in mid to late spring. *Foliage* Leaves small, elliptic, 2½-4in (6-10cm) long, light to mid green. Some yellow autumn colour. *Stem* Strong, upright, becoming branching with age, eventually forming a very dense, branching twiggy framework. Dark green to green-brown. Medium growth rate. *Fruit* Small green fruit capsules in late summer.
Hardiness Tolerates winter temperatures down to −13°F (−25°C).
Soil Requirements Most soil types, tolerates alkaline conditions provided depth of topsoil

Magnolia × loebneri **'Leonard Messel' in flower**

is adequate.

Sun/Shade aspect Prefers full sun, tolerates light shade. As a precaution against frost damage in spring, plant shrub in an area where it does not get early morning sun, so that flowers thaw out slowly, thus limiting tissue damage.

Pruning None required. If desired, can be pruned as a single-stem tree with good results.

Propagation and nursery production From layers or semi-ripe cuttings taken in early summer. Purchase container-grown or root-balled (balled-and-burlapped). Best planting heights 1½-3ft (60cm-1m).

Problems Some varieties, such as *M. kobus*, are slow to come into flower and can take as long as 15 years to produce a full display.

Varieties of interest *M. kobus* (Northern Japanese Magnolia, Kobus Magnolia) White, fragrant flowers produced only after 10-15 years from date of planting. *M. × loebneri* A cross between *M. kobus* and *M. stellata*, which from an early age produces a profusion of multi-petalled, fragrant, white flowers in early to mid spring. Does well on all soil types, including alkaline. Reaches two-thirds average height and spread. Of garden origin. *M. × l. 'Leonard Messel'* Fragrant, multi-petalled flowers are deep pink in bud, opening to lilac-pink. Said to be a cross between *M. kobus* and *M. stellata 'Rosea'*. Of garden origin, from Nymans Gardens, Sussex, England. *M. × l. 'Merrill'* Large, white, star-shaped, fragrant flowers produced from an early age on a shrub two-thirds average height and spread. Raised in the Arnold Arboretum, Massachusetts, USA. *M. salicifolia* White, fragrant, star-shaped flowers with 6 narrow petals in mid spring. Slightly more than average height but slightly less spread, forming either a large shrub or small tree. Leaves, bark and wood are lemon-scented if bruised.

Magnolia × loebneri 'Merrill' in flower

Average height and spread
Five years
6x6ft (2x2m)
Ten years
13x13ft (4x4m)
Twenty years or at maturity
23x26ft (7x8m)

41

MAGNOLIA × SOULANGIANA

SAUCER MAGNOLIA, TULIP MAGNOLIA
Magnoliaceae
Deciduous
Very popular flowering shrubs, which must be given adequate space to develop. None of the beautiful varieties surpasses the splendour of *M. × soulangiana* itself.

Origin Raised by M. Soulange-Bodin at Fromont, near Paris, France in the early 19th century.

Use As a freestanding shrub or eventually a small tree or for a large shrub border, where adequate space available. All varieties do well as wall-trained shrubs.

Magnolia × soulangiana 'Alba Superba' in flower

Description *Flower* Light pink with purple shading in centre and at base of each petal; flowers produced before leaves in early spring. Flower buds large with hairy outer coat. Some secondary flowering in early summer. *Foliage* Leaves elliptic to ovate, 3-6in (8-15cm) long, light green to grey-green. Some yellow autumn colour. *Stem* Upright, strong when young and light grey-green. In maturity branches become very short, twiggy and almost rubbery in texture, forming a basal skirt. Can be trained as single or multi-stemmed standard trees in favourable areas. Medium rate of growth. *Fruit* Insignificant.

Hardiness Tolerates 4°F (−15°C).

Soil Requirements Does well on heavy clay soils and other types, except extremely alkaline areas which will lead to chlorosis.

Sun/Shade aspect Must be planted away from early morning sun. Otherwise flowers frozen by late spring frosts thaw too quickly and cell damage causes browning.

Pruning None required, but best to remove any small crossing branches in winter to prevent rubbing.

Propagation and nursery production From

layers or semi-ripe cuttings taken in early summer. Purchase container-grown or root-balled (balled-and-burlapped). *M.* × *soulangiana* easy to find but some varieties best sought from specialist nurseries. Best planting heights 2-4ft (60cm-1.2m).

Problems Can take up to 5 years or more to flower well.

Varieties of interest *M.* × *s.* *'Alba Superba'* syn. *M.* × *s.* *'Alba'* Large, scented, pure white, erect, tulip-shaped flowers, flushed purple at petal bases. Growth upright and strong, but forms slightly less spread than the parent. *M.* × *s.* *'Alexandrina'* Large, upright, white flowers with purple-flushed petal bases. A good, vigorous, upright, free-flowering variety, sometimes difficult to obtain. *M.* × *s.* *'Amabilis'* Ivory white, tulip-shaped flowers, flushed light purple at bases of inner petals. Upright habit. May have to be obtained from specialist nurseries. *M.* × *s.* *'Brozzonii'* Large, longer than average, white flowers with purple shading at base. Not always available in garden centres and nurseries. *M.* × *s.* *'Lennei'* Flowers goblet-shaped with fleshy petals rose purple outside, creamy white stained purple on inner sides, in mid to late spring; in some seasons, repeated limited flowering in autumn. Broad, ovate leaves, up to 25-30cm (10-12in) long. *M.* × *s.* *'Lennei Alba'* Ivory white, extremely beautiful goblet-shaped flowers presenting themelves upright along branches. May need to be obtained from specialist nurseries. Slightly more than average spread. *M.* × *s.* *'Picture'* Purple outer colouring to petals, white inner sides. Flowers erectly borne, often appearing early in the shrub's lifespan. Leaves up to 10in (25cm) long. Somewhat upright branches, reaching less than average spread. Best sought from specialist nurseries. *M.* × *s.* *'Speciosa'* White flowers with very little purple shading, leaves smaller than average. Slightly less than average height and spread. Best sought from specialist nurseries.

Average height and spread
Five years
6x6ft (2x2m)
Ten years
13x13ft (4x4m)
Twenty years or at maturity
26x26ft (8x8m)

MAGNOLIA STELLATA

STAR MAGNOLIA, STAR-FLOWERED MAGNOLIA
Magnoliaceae
Deciduous
A well-loved, exceptionally beautiful early spring-flowering garden shrub.

Origin From Japan.
Use As a feature shrub in its own right, or for a large shrub border.
Description *Flower* Slightly scented, white, narrow, strap-like, multi-petalled, star-shaped flowers, 2-2½in (5-6cm) across, borne in early spring before leaves. Usually flowers within two years of planting. *Foliage* Leaves medium-sized, elliptic, 2-4in (5-10cm) long, light green, giving some yellow autumn colouring. *Stem* Upright when young, quickly branching and spreading, to form a dome-

Average height and spread
Five years
2½x3ft (80cmx1m)
Ten years
5x6ft (1.5x2m)
Twenty years or at maturity
8x12ft (2.5x3.5m)

shaped shrub slightly wider than it is high. Grey-green. Slow growth rate. *Fruit* Insignificant.

Hardiness Tolerates 4°F (−15°C).

Soil Requirements Any soil type except extremely alkaline.

Sun/Shade aspect Full sun to light shade. As a precaution against frost damage in spring, plant in a position where the shrub will not get early morning sun, so allowing frozen flowers to thaw out slowly, and incur less tissue damage and browning.

Pruning None required.

Propagation and nursery production From layers or cuttings taken in early summer. Purchase container-grown or root-balled (balled-and-burlapped). Normally available from garden centres and nurseries, especially in spring when in flower. Best planting heights 1¼-2½ft (40-80cm).

Problems Young plants when purchased may look small and misshapen due to their slow growth, and can seem expensive, but the investment is well worthwhile.

Varieties of interest *M. s. 'King Rose'* A variety with good pink flowers. *M. s. 'Rosea'* Star-shaped flowers deep pink in bud, opening to flushed pink. *M. s. 'Royal Star'* Slightly larger white flowers with numerous petals making a very full star shape. *M. s. 'Rubra'*

Magnolia stellata in flower

Flowers multi-petalled and purple-pink, deeper colouring while in bud. Rather scarce. *M. s. 'Water Lily'* Larger flowers with more petals. Extremely attractive, but usually a little weaker in constitution than the parent.

MAHONIA JAPONICA

KNOWN BY BOTANICAL NAME
Berberidaceae
Evergreen
A delightful feature for any average-sized garden for its scented flowers in winter.

Origin From Japan.

Use As a freestanding shrub in its own right, for mass planting or for large shrub borders.

Description *Flower* Terminal racemes of yellow to lemon yellow, very fragrant flowers, at first upright, but becoming weeping with age. *Foliage* Leaves large, broad, pinnate, with 5-9 pairs of diamond-shaped leaflets up to 8-10in (20-25cm) long. Dark green on acid soil, red-green on alkaline, with soft spines at end of each lobe of leaf axil. *Stem* Upright when young, with spiny leaflets at each leaf axil, becoming spreading with age, forming a round-topped, slightly spreading shrub. Medium growth rate. *Fruit* Racemes of blue-black fruits follow flowers in late winter and early spring.

Hardiness Tolerates winter temperatures down to −13°F (−25°C).

Soil Requirements Any soil but foliage colour is affected by alkalinity and acidity.

Sun/Shade aspect Prefers medium or light shade, tolerates full sun.

Pruning All flowering terminals should be pruned back each year after fruiting to encourage branching and increase flowering the following year. Any lax shoots which come out above general shape should be cut back.

Propagation and nursery production From semi-ripe cuttings taken in early summer. Purchase container-grown. Easy to find. Best planting heights 1¼-3ft (40cm-1m).

Problems None.

Varieties of interest *M. bealei* Differs from *M. japonica* by having shorter, stouter, more erect flowers and shorter, rounder and slightly concave, red-green, pinnate leaves. Has generally been superseded by *M. japonica* for garden use, but may be offered as an alternative.

Mahonia japonica
in flower

Average height and spread
Five years
5x5½ft (1.5x1.8m)
Ten years
8x9ft (2.5x2.8m)
Twenty years or at maturity
12x10ft (3.5x3m)

45

MALUS Green-leaved, flowering varieties

FLOWERING CRAB, CRAB, CRAB APPLE
Rosaceae
Deciduous
Very attractive and interesting, spring-flowering trees.

Origin Mostly of garden origin; a few direct species.

Use As medium-sized flowering trees for medium and large gardens. Best grown singly.

Description *Flower* White, pink-white or bi-coloured pink and white flowers 1½in (4cm) across, individually or in clusters of 5-7 flowers, producing a mass display. *Foliage* Green, ovate, 2in (5cm) long, tooth-edged, giving some yellow autumn colour. *Fruit* Normally green to yellow-green and of little attraction. *Stem* Purple-red to purple-green. Upright when young, quickly spreading and branching, forming a round-topped tree.

Hardiness Tolerates −13°F (−25°C).

Soil Requirements Most soil conditions; dislikes waterlogging.

Sun/Shade aspect Full sun to light shade, preferring full sun.

Pruning None required except removal of crossing and obstructing branches.

Propagation and nursery production From budding or grafting on to wild apple understock. Plant bare-rooted or container-grown. Can be purchased from 3ft (1m) up to 10ft (3m). Trees of 13-16ft (4-5m) occasionally available, but recommended planting heights 5½-8ft (1.8-2.5m).

Problems Can suffer from severe attacks of apple mildew and lesser attacks of apple scab.

Varieties of interest *M. baccata* White flowers up to 1½in (4cm) across in mid spring, followed by bright red, globe-shaped fruits. One-third more than average height and spread. From eastern Asia and north China. Normally sold in the form *M. baccata var. mandshurica,* which has slightly larger fruits. *M. Coronaria 'Charlottae'* Foliage ovate and coarsely toothed, up to 4in (10cm) long and 2in (5cm) wide. Semi-double, fragrant flowers borne singly or in twos or threes up to 1½in (4cm) across; attractive mother-of-pearl to mid pink colouring. Fruits large, green-yellow, not conspicuous. *M. 'Evereste'* A dwarf, mass-flowering variety. Flowers pink-white. One-third average height and spread. Not readily available, but not impossible to find. *M. floribunda* A pendulous variety, branches on mature trees reaching to ground. Can also be grown as large shrub. Flowers rose red in bud, opening to pink, finally fading to white, produced in mid to late spring in great profusion. Foliage smaller than most, ovate and deeply toothed. *M. 'Hillieri'* Somewhat weak constitution but worth consideration. Flowers semi-double, 1½in (4cm) wide, crimson-red in bud, opening to bright pink. Slightly pendulous habit.

Very thin wood. *M. hupehensis* Fragrant flowers soft pink in bud, opening to white. Fruits yellow with red tints. Two-thirds average height and spread. Somewhat upright in habit. From China and Japan. *M.'Katherine'* Semi-double flowers, pink in bud, finally white. Bright red fruits with yellow flushing. Two-thirds average height and spread with a globular head. Not readily found in production, but worth some research. *M. 'Lady Northcliffe'* Carmine-red buds opening to white with blush shading. Fruits small, yellow and round. Two-thirds average height and spread. Not always available. *M.'Magdeburgensis'* A tree similar to a cultivated apple. Flowers deep red in bud, opening to blush-pink, finally becoming white. Fruits light green to green-yellow and unimportant. Two-thirds average height and spread. Not readily available, but not impossible to find. *M. sargentii* Foliage oblong with three lobes, up to 2½in (6cm) long. Some yellow autumn colour. Flowers pure white with greenish centres in clusters of 5 and 6; petals overlap. Fruits bright red. Very floriferous. Shrubby and reaches only one-third average height and spread, possibly more when grown as a standard tree. May be best grown as large shrub, though good effect when trained into small tree. Originating in Japan. *M. × scheideckeri* Coarsely toothed, small, elliptic to ovate leaves, sometimes with 3-5 lobes. Flowers pink to deep rose in clusters of 3-6. Growth very slender. Fruits yellow and round. A shrubby variety reaching one-third average height and spread. *M. 'Snow Cloud'* A relatively new variety of upright habit, reaching average height but less than average spread. Profuse white double flowers, opening from pink buds, in mid spring. Fruits inconspicuous. Foliage dark green with autumn tints. *M. spectabilis* Grey-green foliage

Malus floribunda
in flower

susceptible to apple scab. Flowers rosy red in bud, opening to pale blush pink, up to 2in (5cm) across and borne in clusters of 6-8 in early spring. Fruits yellow and globe-shaped. From China. *M. 'Strathmore'* Light green foliage. A profusion of pale pink flowers.

Malus hupehensis **in flower**

Round-topped. *M. toringoides* Foliage ovate to lanceolate up to 3in(8cm) long. Deeply lobed new foliage; that produced on older wood is less indented. Pastel autumn colours. Flowers light pink in bud opening to creamy-white, produced in clusters of 6-8. Fruit globe-shaped, yellow with scarlet flushing. Two-thirds average height and spread with a graceful, flat-headed effect. From China. *M. transitoria* Small-lobed foliage with small pink-white flowers and rounded yellow fruits. Excellent autumn colour. Two-thirds average height and spread. From north-west China. *M. trilobata* Leaves maple-shaped, deeply lobed, three-sectioned, mid to dark green with good autumn colour. White flowers, followed by infrequently produced yellow fruits. Originating in Eastern Mediterranean and north-eastern Greece. Two-third average height and spread. Scarce in production and will have to be sought from specialist nurseries. *M. 'Van Eseltine'* Flowers rose-scarlet in bud, opening to shell pink, semi-double. Small yellow fruits. Two-thirds average height and spread, slightly columnar habit.

Average height and spread
Five years
13x5ft (4x1.5m)
Ten years
20x10ft (6x3m)
Twenty years or at maturity
26x20ft (8x6m)

PHILADELPHUS Low-growing varieties

MOCK ORANGE
Philadelphaceae
Deciduous
Useful low-growing, scented summer-flowering shrubs. These are often mistakenly given the common name Syringa.

Origin Most varieties of garden origin.
Use For planting singly, for medium to large shrub borders, or for mass planting.
Description *Flower* White, often fragrant flowers, ¾in (2cm) wide, single or double, depending on variety, borne in midsummer. *Foliage* Leaves ovate and slightly tooth-edged, 1½-4in (4-10cm) long, light to mid green, giving good yellow autumn colour. Some varieties with variegation. *Stem* Upright, forming an upright, round-topped shrub. Grey-green. Medium to fast growth rate. *Fruit* Insignificant.
Hardiness Tolerates winter temperatures down to −13°F (−25°C).
Soil Requirements Any soil including both alkaline and acid types.
Sun/Shade aspect Full sun through to medium shade.
Pruning With established plants 3 years old or more remove one-third of oldest flowering shoots after flowering.
Propagation and nursery production From semi-ripe cuttings taken in early summer or hardwood cuttings in winter. Plant bare-rooted or container-grown. Best planting heights 8in-1½ft (20-50cm).
Problems Commonly harbours blackfly which can transfer to other garden crops.
Varieties of interest *P. 'Boule d'Argent'* Double white, scented flowers, compact habit. Hard to find but worth the attempt. *P. coronarius 'Variegatus'* Single to semi-

Average height and spread
Five years
2½x2½ft (80x80cm)
Ten years
3x3ft (1x1m)
Twenty years or at maturity
4x4ft (1.2x1.2m)

Philadelphus 'Manteau d'Hermine' in flower

Philadelphus coronarius 'Variegatus' in leaf

double, white, scented flowers, early summer. Grey-green leaves with bold, creamy white margins. Light dappled shade essential; strong sunlight scorches and deforms the shrub. *P. 'Manteau d'Hermine'* Double white to creamy white, very fragrant flowers. One of the most popular of low-growing forms. *P. microphyllus* Single, very small, white, scented flowers on very twiggy growth. *P. 'Silver Showers'* Masses of white, scented double flowers on upright, graceful stems.

PHILADELPHUS Medium height varieties

MOCK ORANGE
Philadelphaceae
Deciduous
A useful group of summer-flowering fragrant shrubs.

Origin Most varieties of garden origin.
Use For planting singly, or in medium to large shrub borders, or for mass planting.
Description *Flower* White, often fragrant flowers, ¾-1½in (2-4cm) wide, single or double, depending on variety, some with purple throat markings, borne in midsummer. *Foliage* Leaves ovate, 1½-4in (4-10cm) long, slightly tooth-edged, light to mid green with good yellow autumn colour. Some varieties variegated. *Stem* Upright, forming an upright, round-topped shrub and grey-green. Medium to fast growth rate. *Fruit* Insignificant.
Hardiness Tolerates winter temperatures down to −13°F (−25°C).

Soil Requirements Most soils, including alkaline and acid types.

Sun/Shade aspect Full sun through to medium shade.

Pruning On established plants 3 years old or more, remove one third of older flowering wood to ground level after flowering.

Propagation and nursery production From semi-ripe cuttings taken in early summer or from hardwood cuttings in winter. Purchase container-grown or bare-rooted. Best planting heights 1¼-2½ft (40-80cm).

Problems Harbours blackfly which can transfer to other garden crops.

Varieties of interest *P. 'Avalanche'* Small, pure white, single, scented flowers borne in profusion. An upright-growing shrub with smaller than average foliage. *P. 'Belle Etoile'* White, single, fragrant flowers with maroon central blotches. *P. 'Erectus'* Pure white, single, scented flowers, very free flowering. Distinct, upright branches. *P. 'Galahad'* Single, scented, white flowers. Stems mahogany-brown in winter. Rather hard to find. *P. 'Innocence'* Single, white, fragrant flowers, foliage sometimes having creamy white variegation. *P. 'Sybille'* Almost square, purple-stained, single, white flowers, orange-scented, on arching branches.

Average height and spread
Five years
3x3ft (1x1m)
Ten years
5x5ft (1.5x1.5m)
Twenty years or at maturity
5x6ft (1.5x2m)

Philadelphus 'Belle Etoile' **in flower**

POTENTILLA

SHRUBBY CINQUEFOIL, BUTTERCUP SHRUB, FIVE FINGER
Rosaceae
Deciduous
Gems of summer-flowering shrubs, offering a wide choice of flower and foliage colour and different heights.

Origin *P. arbuscula* and *P. dahurica* are from the Himalayas, northern China and Siberia. *P. fruticosa* is native to a wide area of the northern hemisphere, but most varieties now of garden origin.
Use Grouped in a border of any size or planted singly. If planted 2ft (60cm) apart makes an informal, low hedge.
Description *Flower* Small, single saucer-shaped flowers, up to 1in (3cm) across, in colours dependent on variety, ranging from white through primrose, yellow, pink, orange and red, borne mainly in midsummer, but from early summer through to early autumn. *Foliage* Leaves cut and lobed, pinnate, with 3, 5 or 7 leaflets, linear to oblong, ½-1in (1-3cm) long, overlapping. Light green to sage green to silver green, depending on variety. Some yellow autumn colour. *Stem* Grey to grey-brown, appearing dead when bare, but quickly producing foliage in spring. Some varieties grow directly upright to form round-topped shrubs. Others are mound-forming, a few almost prostrate. *Fruit* Brown-grey seed-heads formed after flowering.
Hardiness Tolerant of winter temperatures down to −13°F (−25°C).
Soil Requirements Wide range of soils, only distressed by extremely dry, wet or very alkaline conditions.
Sun/Shade aspect Prefers full sun, tolerates

Potentilla dahurica
'Abbotswood'
in flower

Potentilla 'Daydawn'
in flower

mid shade.

Pruning Each year after planting remove one-third of growth, and occasionally cut back older stems to ground level to induce maximum rejuvenation. Very old established, neglected shrubs can either be cut extremely hard, when they will produce new growth, or thinned over a period of years to bring them back into full production.

Propagation and nursery production From softwood or semi-ripe cuttings taken in spring or early summer. Purchase container-grown. Most varieties fairly easy to find. Best planting heights 8in-2ft (20-60cm).

Problems Can appear to have died in winter. If not pruned annually becomes woody.

Varieties of interest *P. arbuscula* Good yellow flowers over a long period, contrasting with grey-green foliage. Forming a bushy mound with arching branches. Slightly less than average height and spread. *P. a. 'Beesii'* syn. *P. fruticosa 'Beesii'*, *P. a. 'Nana Argentea'* Bright golden yellow flowers, contrasting well with bright silvery-grey foliage. Forms a flattish mound. Reaches one-third average height and spread. *P. dahurica 'Abbotswood'* Pure white flowers, grey-green foliage. Mound-forming. Reaching two-thirds average height and spread. *P. d. 'Manchu'* syn. *P. mandshurica fruticosa* White flowers, grey-green foliage. Very low and carpet-forming, reaching only 8in (20cm) in height with spread of 2ft (60cm). *P. d. 'Mount Everest'* syn. *P. fruticosa 'Mount Everest'* Pure white, large flowers. Strong-growing, making a round shrub. *P. d. var. veitchii* syn. *P. fruticosa veitchii* Pure white flowers, grey-green foliage. Upright, forming spreading top shape, two-thirds average height with slightly more spread. From western and central China. *P. 'Dart's Golddigger'* Covered in buttercup yellow flowers, against grey-green foliage. Round and bushy. Two-thirds average height and spread. *P. 'Daydawn'* Peach

Potentilla 'Elizabeth'
in flower

pink to cream flowers, which maintain their colour in strong sunlight. Bushy habit. Reaching two-thirds average height and spread. *P. 'Elizabeth'* syn. *P. fruticosa 'Elizabeth'* Covered in large, canary yellow flowers against grey-green foliage background. Bushy habit. Often confused with and sold as *P. arbuscula*. *P. fruticosa* Smaller, yellow flowers covering an upright shrub with much smaller, divided leaves, light green to mid green. Upright habit. *P. 'Jackman's Variety'* Bright golden yellow flowers. Strong, upright-growing shrub with green foliage. One of the best forms for hedging. *P. 'Katherine Dykes'* Covered in primrose yellow flowers, with grey-green foliage. Bushy habit. A strong-growing variety, reaching slightly more than average height and spread. *P. 'Longacre'* Good-sized sulphur yellow flowers, green foliage. Bushy habit. Reaching two-thirds average height and spread. *P. 'Maanelys'* syn. *P. 'Moonlight'* Covered in soft yellow to primrose yellow flowers throughout summer. Grey-green foliage. Upright habit. *P. parvifolia* Covered in small golden yellow flowers. Mid green to dark green foliage. Tight, compact, upright habit, reaching slightly less than average height and equal spread. *P. p. 'Buttercup'* syn. *P. fruticosa 'Buttercup'* Small, deep golden yellow flowers, green foliage. Bushy habit. *P. p. 'Klondike'* syn. *P. fruticosa 'Klondike'* One of the best golden yellow forms. Small green foliage. Upright to bushy in habit. Slightly less than average height and spread. *P. 'Primrose Beauty'* syn. *P. fruticosa 'Primrose Beauty'* Primrose yellow flowers with dark yellow centres. Grey to grey-green foliage. Can be somewhat untidy with its large brown seedheads. Bushy habit. *P. 'Princess'* Flowers softest rose pink. Green foliage. A small shrub of bushy habit, reaching one-third average height and equal spread. **P. 'Red Ace'** Red to orange-red flowers against a finely cut green leaf background. Needs light shade to maintain good red colour. Bushy habit. Reaching two-thirds average height and spread. **P. 'Royal Flush'** Deep rose pink flowers set against largish green leaves. Somewhat susceptible to die-back, especially in wet conditions. May be unreliable. Bushy habit. **P. 'Sanved'** syn. **P. sandudana** Good-sized white flowers, bright green leaves on upright, bushy shrub. **P. 'Sunset'** Orange flowers flecked with brick red. Green foliage. Best in light shade for good colour effect. Bushy habit. **P. 'Tangerine'** Pale copper yellow to tangerine orange-yellow flowers. Requires light shade to maintain flower colour. Bushy habit. Two-thirds average height and spread. **P. 'Tilford Cream'** Creamy white flowers of good size, borne in profusion, with slightly grey-green foliage. Bushy habit. Reaches two-thirds average height and spread. **P. 'Vilmoriniana'** syn. **P. fruticosa 'Vilmoriniana'** Very pretty primrose yellow flowers, attractive silver foliage. Probably found only in specialist nurseries. Can be difficult to establish. Upright, reaching slightly more than average height.

Average height and spread
Five years
2½x2½ft (80x80cm)
Ten years
4x4ft (1.2x1.2m)
Twenty years or at maturity
4x4ft (1.2x1.2m)

PRUNUS Early-flowering Cherries

FLOWERING CHERRY
Rosaceae
Deciduous
Heralds of the spring. Extremely fine flowering trees for early blossom effect.

Origin Of garden origin and hybrid crosses.
Use As small to medium early-flowering trees for any size of garden.

***Prunus 'Okame'* in flower**

Description *Flower* Single flowers, white, shell pink, mid pink or purple-pink dependent on variety, produced on bare branches in great profusion from late winter to early spring, or spring-flowering. *Foliage* Ovate, up to 4in (10cm) long, with toothed edges. Light to mid green with yellow, often spectacular, autumn colour. *Stem* Thin growth, very branching habit, forming either a round-topped and spreading or upright tree, depending on variety. Wood grey to grey-green. Medium rate of growth. *Fruit* Insignificant.

Hardiness Tolerates 4°F (−15°C).

Soil Requirements Most soil conditions; dislikes extremely dry or poor soils.

Sun/Shade aspect Will tolerate full sun to mid shade, preferring light shade.

Pruning None required other than the removal of any crossing or crowded branches. Prune while tree is dormant and treat cuts quickly with pruning compound to prevent fungus disease.

Propagation and nursery production From budding or grafting on to understocks of *P. avium*. Planted bare-rooted or container-grown. Normally sold at 5½-10ft (1.8-3m). Most varieties readily available from general nurseries, but a few must be sought from specialist outlets.

Problems Flower buds may be damaged by birds, in quiet areas, sometimes severely. Young trees can look weak at purchase due to thin growth, but improve after planting.

Varieties of interest *P. 'Accolade'* A cross between *P. sargentii* and *P. subhirtella*. Large clusters of rich pink flowers up to 8in (20cm) across, individual flowers up to 1½in (4cm) across. Good autumn colour. Average height with slightly more spread, branches pendulous in habit on mature trees. *P. 'Hally Jolivette'* A cross between *P. subhirtella* and *P. yedoensis* × *subhirtella*. Thin stems produce clusters of small semi-double, pale pear-

***Prunus* × *yedoensis* in flower**

ly pink flowers through early spring. Predominantly used as a large shrub, later reaching the proportions of a small tree. Raised in the Arnold Arboretum, Massachusetts, USA. *P. × hillieri 'Spire'* A cross between *P. incisa* and *P. sargentii*. Soft pink flowers and good autumn colours. Useful for all sizes of garden. Upright to conical, reaching average height, but basal spread only 10ft (3m). Raised in the Hilliers Nurseries in Winchester, England. *P. incisa* (Fuji Cherry) Foliage small, light green with good autumn colours. Flowers pink in bud, opening to white. Occasionally produces small purple black fruits. Round-topped habit. Best grown as a large shrub, but can be found as a small standard tree. Slightly less than average height and spread. *P. i. 'February Pink'* Flowers slightly earlier than *P. incisa* and with more pink colouring. *P. 'Kursar'* A cross between *P. campanula* and *P. kurilensis*. Profuse, deep pink flowers in mid spring. Young foliage red-bronze; good yellow autumn tints. Forms a small, round-topped tree with interesting dark purple stems. Not readily available, but may be found in specialist nurseries. *P. 'Moerheimii'* syn. *P. incisa 'Moerheimii'* Flowers pink in bud, opening to white with blush pink shading. Round-topped, weeping branches, forming a dome-shaped effect of two-thirds average height and spread. May be difficult to find, and must be sought from specialist nurseries. *P. 'Okame'* A cross between *P. campanulata* and *P. incisa*. A delightful round-topped small tree, early-flowering and reaching two-thirds average height and spread. Profuse crimson-rose flowers in early spring. Good yellow autumn tints. *P. 'Pandora'* Shell pink flowers up to 1in (3cm) across in early spring. Young foliage bronze-red in spring with good yellow autumn colours. Extremely reliable. *P. 'Umineko'* A cross between *P. incisa* and *P. speciosa*. White flowers in mid spring. Good autumn colour. Upright, of average height and two-thirds average spread. *P. × yedoensis* Spectacular masses of almond-scented, blush-white flowers in early spring. Branches slightly pendulous. From Japan, and apparently of garden origin.

Average height and spread
Five years
12x8ft (3.5x2.5m)
Ten years
23x12ft (7x3.5m)
Twenty years or at maturity
30x23ft (9x7m)

PRUNUS SERRULATA
Large-flowering Japanese Cherries

JAPANESE FLOWERING CHERRY
Rosaceae
Deciduous
Very popular, spring-flowering trees, widely planted, with a large range of planting potential.

Origin From Japan.
Use As medium to large flowering trees for spring blossom. Can also be grown as large bushes if suitable plants can be obtained for planting. Well presented in open grass areas as tall shrubs or short trees.

**Prunus 'Kanzan'
in flower**

Description *Flower* A profusion of dark pink, white or cream, double or single flowers depending on variety, in late spring. *Foliage* Ovate to oval leaves, 3in (8cm) long with toothed edges. Light green to mid green. Yellow or orange autumn colour depending on variety. *Stem* Grey-green to grey-brown. Upright and round-topped or spreading, depending on variety. *Fruit* Insignificant.

Hardiness Tolerates temperatures down to −13°F (−25°C).

Soil Requirements Most soil conditions, but shows signs of distress on extremely poor soils.

Sun/Shade aspect Full sun to light shade.

Pruning None required other than to confine growth as necessary. Crossing branches or limbs can be removed in winter and the cuts treated with pruning compound to prevent fungus diseases.

Propagation and nursery production From budding or grafting. Normally supplied bare-rooted or container-grown from 5-10ft (1.5-3m). Larger trees occasionally available, but often slow to establish and superseded by younger trees. Most varieties readily available from garden centres and general nurseries.

Problems Some varieties, particularly *P. 'Kanzan'* can suffer from silver-leaf virus. There is no cure and affected trees must be burned to prevent further contamination.

Varieties of interest *Prunus 'Asano'* syn. *P. serrulata var. geraldiniae* Large clusters of double deep pink flowers in mid spring. Leaves light green-bronze when young, an attractive contrast with the flowers. Two-thirds average height and spread. Not readily available. *P. 'Fudanzakura'* syn. *P. serrulata var. fudanzakura* Single white flowers, pink in bud, from late winter to early spring during mild periods. Young leaves coppery-red to red-brown in spring. Difficult to find in commercial production. *P. 'Hisakura'* Large, double or semi-double, pale pink flowers. Young leaves brown-bronze in colour. A very old variety, often confused with *P. 'Kanzan'*. *P. 'Hokusai'* Clusters of semi-double, pale pink flowers in mid spring. A round-topped tree with wide-spreading branches. *P. 'Ichiyo'* Double, shell-pink flowers with frilled edges in mid spring. Young foliage bronze-green. Upright habit. Relatively easy to find from specialist nurseries. *P. 'Imose'* Flowers double, mauve-pink, produced in hanging, loose clusters in mid spring. Young foliage copper-coloured, becoming bright green with good yellow autumn colour. Irregularly produces small, round, black fruits. Difficult to find. *P. 'Kanzan'* Very large clusters of double, purple-pink flowers produced in great profusion in mid spring. Young growth copper-red to red-brown, becoming dark green. Good autumn colours. Often confused with *P. 'Hisakura'* but they are distinct varieties, though similar in effect. *P. 'Ojochin'* Single flowers up to 2in (5cm) across in mid spring, pale pink in bud opening to pink-white in long hanging clusters of 7 or 8 florets. Young foliage bronze-brown becoming leathery and dark green with age. *P. 'Pink Perfection'* Pale pink flowers in mid to late spring. Rounded, fairly open habit. Young leaves bronze. Good yellow autumn tints. *P. 'Shimidsu Sakura'* syn. *P. serrulata var. longipes* Flowers double, pink in bud opening to pure white and hanging in clusters along the undersides of all branches in mid to late spring. Young foliage bright green, attractive. Good yellow autumn colours. Wide and spreading, forming a broad, flattened crown. *P. 'Shirofugen'* Flowers purple-pink in bud, aging through light pink to white. Foliage coppery when young, becoming light green. Good autumn tints. Forms a round-topped tree initially, spreading with age. *P. 'Shirotae'* syn. *P. 'Mount Fuji'*

Prunus 'Tai Haku' **in flower**

Prunus 'Ukon'
in flower

**Average height
and spread**
Five years
12x8ft (3.5x2.5m)
Ten years
23x16ft (7x5m)
*Twenty years
or at maturity*
25x25ft (8x8m)

Single or semi-double flowers up to 2in (5cm) across, pure white and fragrant. Young foliage light green; leaves have a distinctive fringed edge. Wide-spreading habit. Horizontal branches dipping sometimes to the ground. *P. 'Shosar'* Single, clear pink flowers in early to mid spring. Good orange-yellow autumn colours. Upright, pyramidal habit. *P. 'Tai Haku'* (Great White Cherry) Single, pure white flowers up to 2in (5cm) across, produced in great profusion in mid-spring. Young foliage copper-red. Spreading branches. Can be grown as large shrub or tree, and extremely attractive in both forms. *P. 'Taoyama Zakura'* Fragrant, semi-double, pale pink flowers in mid spring whitening with age. Good red-brown to copper-coloured young foliage. Low-growing with spreading habit. Relatively difficult to find in commercial production. *P. 'Ukon'* (Green Cherry) Hanging clusters of semi-double, pale green to green-yellow or cream flowers in mid spring, best seen against a background of clear blue sky. Interesting autumn foliage colours of red, yellow and orange.

PRUNUS TRILOBA (Prunus triloba multiplex)

KNOWN BY BOTANICAL NAME
Rosaceae
Deciduous
An attractive, spring-flowering, large shrub or small mop-headed tree.

Origin From China, of garden origin.
Use As a freestanding, large flowering shrub of attractive shape and performance. Good as background in a large shrub border. Can be trained as an attractive small mop-headed tree.
Description *Flower* Double, rosette-shaped, peach-pink flowers of good size borne on entire length of bare stems in mid spring. *Foliage* Leaves ovate, 1½-2½in (4-6cm) long, tooth-edged, mid green giving some yellow autumn colour. *Stem* Upright when young, becoming spreading and pendulous with age, forming a round-topped, large, mound-shaped shrub. Mahogany-brown. Medium to fast growth rate. *Fruit* Insignificant.
Hardiness Tolerates 4°F (−15°C).
Soil Requirements Any soil.
Sun/Shade aspect Full sun to light shade.
Pruning Cut back one-third of old flowering shoots moderately hard after flowering to induce new flowering wood for subsequent years.
Propagation and nursery production From semi-ripe cuttings taken in early summer, or from budding or grafting. Standards normally budded or grafted on to stems of *P. avium*. Purchase root-balled (balled-and-burlapped) or container-grown. Best planting heights 1¼-2½ft (40-80cm).
Problems Young plants do not show their full potential.

Average height and spread
Five years
4x4ft (1.2x1.2m)
Ten years
5½x5½ft (1.8x1.8m)
Twenty years or at maturity
8x8ft (2.5x2.5m)

Prunus triloba in flower

RHODODENDRON Dwarf hybrids

DWARF RHODODENDRON
Ericaceae
Evergreen
Among the most beautiful spring-flowering shrubs, but requiring specific soil conditions.

Origin Varieties listed are mostly of garden origin.

Use As low, dwarf, spring-flowering shrubs for use with heathers and dwarf conifers. Ideal for growing in tubs not less than 2½ft (80cm) in diameter and 2ft (60cm) in depth; use good lime-free potting medium. Very good for medium to large rock gardens and for mass planting.

Description *Flower* Borne in small trusses in a wide range of colours from blue, through pink, purple, red and white from early, mid or late spring, depending on variety. *Foliage* Leaves generally small, round to ovate, ½-1¼in (1-3.5cm) long, dark green with glossy upper surfaces and dull undersides. *Stem* Very short, branching habit, forming a dome-shaped, low, spreading shrub. Slow growth rate. *Fruit* Insignificant.

Hardiness Tolerates 4°F (−15°C).

Soil Requirements Neutral to acid soils. Dislikes any alkalinity or waterlogging.

Sun/Shade aspect Prefers light shade, tolerates from full sun to mid shade.

Pruning None required.

Propagation and nursery production From semi-ripe cuttings taken early to mid summer. Purchase container-grown or root-balled (balled-and-burlapped). Most varieties fairly easy to find, especially when in flower. Best planting heights 8in-2ft (20-60cm).

Problems Buds susceptible to insect attacks; remove damaged buds. Severe wind chill may

Rhododendron 'Blue Diamond' **in flower**

damage foliage and buds.

Varieties of interest *R. 'Bluebird'* Violet-blue trusses borne in mid spring on dwarf, round, tight, small-leaved shrub. *R. 'Blue Diamond'* Intense lavender-blue flowers borne in mid spring in small terminal clusters on slow-growing, tight shrub. *R. 'Blue Tit'* Funnel-shaped lavender-blue flowers in small terminal clusters, colour deepening with age. Borne in mid spring. Dense mould-shaped shrub. *R. 'Bow Bells'* Flowers wide and bell-shaped, deep cerise in bud, opening to soft pink, richer pink on outer side. Trusses loosely presented in mid to late spring on compact shrub. Young foliage copper. *R. 'Bric-a-Brac'* Pure white, wide open flowers, 2½in (6cm) across, with chocolate anthers, borne early to mid spring. *R. 'Carmen'* Large, bell-shaped flowers, 1¾-2in (4.5-5cm) across, dark crimson with pale pink throats in mid spring. Larger leaves than most dwarf forms, up to 2-2½in (5-6cm) long, ovate, covering a dwarf, prostrate shrub. *R. 'Elisabeth Hobbie'* Trusses of 5-10, almost translucent, bell-shaped, scarlet red flowers in mid spring. *R. 'Elizabeth'* Flowers trumpet-shaped, 2½-2¾in (6-7cm) across, rich dark red, borne in mid to late spring. Slightly taller than most varieties, with spreading habit. *R. 'Humming Bird'* Hanging flowers, scarlet-red with scarlet inner shading, borne in early-spring. Dome-shaped, dwarf shrub of compact habit. *R. 'Moonstone'* Rose-crimson buds, opening to cream and pale primrose bell-shaped flowers in mid to late spring. Low, dome-shaped shrub. *R. 'Pink Drift'* Flowers lavender-rose in small clusters, produced in late spring. Foliage small, grey-green and aromatic. Good for rock gardens and other areas where a low, very compact, shrub is required. *R. 'Scarlet Wonder'* Trumpet-shaped flowers, ruby red with frilly margins borne in late spring. A dwarf shub, forming a tight mound of close foliage. *R. 'Yellow Hammer'* Bright yellow flowers, pro-

**Average height
and spread**
Five years
2x2ft (60x60cm)
Ten years
2½x3ft (80cmx1m)
*Twenty years
or at maturity*
3x5ft (1x1.5m)

duced in pairs at terminal and axillary buds in mid spring, occasionally also in autumn. Upright, narrow habit.

RHODODENDRON Large-flowering hybrids

KNOWN BY BOTANICAL NAME
Ericaceae
Evergreen
Well-loved and very handsome spring-flowering shrubs.

Origin Crosses from parent plants gathered from throughout the northern hemisphere, many hybridized and of garden origin.
Use As a freestanding shrub on its own or for mass planting; extremely good for accentuating a landscape design. Can be grown in containers for some years provided they are not less than 2½ft (80cm) in diameter and 2ft (60cm) in depth; use good lime-free potting medium.
Description *Flower* Large trusses of bell-shaped flowers up to 6in (15cm) across the truss and 7-8in (18-20cm) long, in colours ranging from white, through pink, to blue and red, depending on variety. Some flowers multicoloured or with petal markings. Mid spring to early summer. *Foliage* Leaves ovate, medium to large, from 4-8in (10-20cm) depending on variety, glossy dark green upper surface with duller, grey-green undersides. Leathery textured. *Stem* Upright, strong shoots when young, grey-green to dark green aging to grey-brown. Becoming branching and in some cases arching, forming a round-topped shrub with base slightly wider than top. Medium growth rate. *Fruit* May produce brown-grey seedheads which should be removed.
Hardiness Tolerates 4°F (−15°C).
Soil Requirements Neutral to acid soil. Dislikes any alkalinity.

Rhododendron
'Britannia' **in flower**

64

Sun/Shade aspect Prefers light shade, but tolerates full sun through to deep shade, if adequate moisture is available.

Pruning None required but large, mature shrubs can be reduced in size after flowering by cutting back even to very old wood.

Propagation and nursery production From grafting. Purchase root-balled (balled-and-burlapped) or container-grown. Fairly easy to find, although some varieties, especially when in flower, will be found only in specialist nurseries. Best planting heights 1¼-2½ft (40-80cm). Shrubs up to 6ft (2m) may be moved if required.

Problems Acid soil is essential and it is useless to attempt to grow rhododendrons on alkaline soils. Flower buds may be attacked by insects which are extremely difficult to control; remove affected buds to reduce infestation in future years.

Varieties of interest *R. 'Bagshot Ruby'* Large trusses, dense in formation, consisting of ruby red wide-mouthed funnel-shaped flowers, flowering late spring. *R. 'Betty Wormald'* Deep crimson in bud. Deep rose pink, funnel-shaped flowers with a wide, wavy-edged mouth and some maroon to black-crimson spots on inner sides. Large to very large trusses. Late spring. *R. 'Blue Peter'* Flower trusses conical and tightly formed, borne in late spring. Funnel-shaped flowers have frilled edges and are cobalt blue, aging to white in throat with ring of maroon spots. Strong-growing. *R. 'Britannia'* Flowers gloxinia-shaped, scarlet-crimson and in tight trusses, borne in late spring. Forms a round shrub, which in time also forms a low ground skirt. Slightly less than average height. *R. 'Countess of Athlone'* Wide, funnel-shaped, wavy-edged flowers in late spring. Buds purple, opening to mauve with yellow to green-yellow basal markings in cone-shaped trusses. *R. 'Countess of Derby'* Buds pink, opening to pink but intensifying with age. Flowers wide, funnel-shaped, with red-brown spots and streaks inside, borne in tight cone-shaped trusses in late spring. *R. 'Cynthia'* Strong-growing variety and quick to form a dome-shaped shrub. Rose-crimson, cone-shaped large flowers, with black-crimson markings, borne in late spring. *R. 'Earl of Donoughmore'* Good-sized trusses of bright red flowers with orange glow in late spring. *R. 'Fastuosum Flore Pleno'* Somewhat lax trusses of rich mauve funnel-shaped flowers with ring of brown-crimson markings on inner side and wavy edges, borne in late spring. Forming a dome-shaped shrub of good proportions. *R. 'General Eisenhower'* Large trusses of carmine-red flowers in late spring. A well-shaped shrub. *R. 'Goldsworth Orange'* Good-sized trusses of orange to pale orange flowers, each tinged with apricot pink in early summer. A somewhat low, spreading bush, reaching two-thirds average height and average spread. *R. 'Goldsworth Yellow'* Round trusses of funnel-shaped flowers, pink in bud and primrose yellow with brown mark-ings on inner surface when open in late spring. Good foliage on dome-shaped, spreading shrub. *R. 'Gomer Waterer'* Round trusses of good-sized funnel-shaped flowers, divided at the mouth; white with pale mauve flush towards outer edges and mustard coloured blotches at base of petals. Late spring to early summer. Good-sized shrub with attractive leathery, oval to oblong foliage. *R. 'Kluis Sensation'* Large flowers, bright scarlet with darker red spots on outer edges, in late spring. *R. 'Kluis Triumph'* Deep red flowers in good-sized trusses borne on large shrub in late spring. *R. 'Lord Roberts'* Round trusses of funnel-shaped flowers, deep crimson with black markings on inner side, late spring to early summer. Upright habit. *R. 'Madame de Bruin'* Cone-shaped trusses of cerise-red flowers in late spring. Good foliage on strong-growing shrub. *R. 'Moser's Maroon'* Maroon-red flowers with darker inner markings in each truss, in late spring to early summer. New foliage copper. Strong-growing, upright habit. *R. 'Mrs. G.W. Leak'* Lax, conical trusses of wide, funnel-shaped flowers, light rosy pink mottling, becoming darker towards base of tubes. Black-brown and crimson markings. Late spring. *R. 'Old Port'* Thick trusses of wide, funnel-shaped flowers, plum-coloured with black-crimson markings, in late spring to early summer. Strong-growing, large leaves. *R. 'Pink Pearl'* Large cone-shaped trusses of wide-mouthed, funnel-shaped flowers in late spring. Rose pink buds, opening to lilac-pink flowers. Outer margins becoming white with age. Large, strong-growing, upright shrub. One of the most widely planted varieties. *R. ponticum* Mauve to lilac-pink, tubular flowers in good-sized, slightly open trusses, borne in late spring. A large, round shrub, extremely useful for windbreaks and hedges. Can be invasive in woodland areas. *R. p. 'Variegatum'* Purple

Rhododendron 'Pink Pearl' in flower

flower trusses in late spring. Foliage grey-green with white variegation. Reaches two-thirds average height and spread. **R. *'Purple Splendour'*** Good-shaped trusses of funnel-shaped, wide-mouthed flowers in late spring to early summer. Rich royal purple-blue with black embossed markings on purple-brown background. Strong-growing, upright branches. **R. *'Sappho'*** Cone-shaped trusses of wide-mouthed funnel-shaped flowers in late spring. Buds mauve, opening to pure white, with rich purple overlaid with black blotch on inner side. Open, round shrub. **R. *'Susan'*** Large trusses of blue-mauve flowers with darker outer edges and purple spots within, in mid to late spring. A strong-growing shrub. **R. *'Unique'*** Flower trusses dome-shaped, creamy white with pinkish shading and crimson spots within, in late spring. Interesting small foliage on dome-shaped shrub, reaching two-thirds average height and spread.

Average height and spread
Five years
4x5ft (1.2x1.5m)
Ten years
6x8ft (2x2.5m)
Twenty years or at maturity
10x13ft (3x4m)

RHODODENDRON Low-growing species

DWARF RHODODENDRON
Ericaceae
Evergreen
A varied range of spring-flowering shrubs for use on acid soils.

Origin Mostly from northern hemisphere, with a wide range of individual locations.
Use As dwarf, spring-flowering shrubs for use with heathers and dwarf conifers, particularly for medium to large rock gardens. Can be grown in tubs not less than 2½ft (80cm) across and 2ft (60cm) deep; use good, lime-free potting medium.
Description *Flower* Small trusses of flowers in

Rhododendron 'Praecox' in flower

Rhododendron
racemosum **in flower**

colours ranging through yellow, blue, purple, pink, red and white. From early to late spring. *Foliage* Leaves round to ovate, ¼-1¾in (5mm-2.5cm) long, dark green or grey, dependent on variety, with glossy upper surfaces and duller undersides. *Stem* Very short, branching habit, forming a dome-shaped, low, spreading shrub. Slow growth rate. *Fruit* Insignificant.

Hardiness Tolerates 4°F (−15°C).

Soil Requirements Neutral to acid soils, dislikes any alkalinity and waterlogging.

Sun/Shade aspect Prefers light shade, tolerates full sun to mid shade.

Pruning Generally requires no pruning. Slow-growing.

Propagation and nursery production From semi-ripe cuttings taken early to mid summer. Purchase root-balled (balled-and-burlapped) or container-grown. Most varieties fairly easy to find. Best planting heights 8in-2ft (20-60cm).

Rhododendron
yakushimanum
in flower

Problems May be subject to insect attacks; remove damaged buds. Flower buds and foliage may be damaged by very severe wind chill.

Varieties of interest *R. ferrugineum* (Alpen Rose of Switzerland) Trusses of small, tubular, rose-crimson flowers in early summer. Red underside to foliage. Flat, dome-shaped shrub of spreading habit. *R. hirsutum* Tubular, rose-pink flowers in clusters in early summer, stems and leaves fringed with bristles. Dwarf, compact, many branched small alpine shrub, two-thirds mature height and spread. *R. impeditum* Purple-blue, funnel-shaped flowers in mid to late spring, produced on low, very small-leaved mound of scaly branches. Dwarf alpine reaching one-third average height and spread. *R. moupinense* Sweet-scented, pink to deep rose, funnel-shaped flowers in late winter, early spring; foliage ovate to elliptic with scaly undersides. Small shrub with bristly branches. May need some protection from east winds while in flower. *R. obtusum 'Amoenum Coccineum'* Carmine-rose flowers, foliage glossy green, oval. Low-growing, thickly branched, spreading shrub, branches being covered in hairs. Semi-evergreen in some situations. *R. pemakoense* Flowers funnel-shaped, lilac-pink to purple, profusely borne in early to mid spring, needing some protection from frost when in bud and flower. A variety reaching one-third mature height and spread, suckering as it goes and producing small, very low-spreading carpet. *R. 'Praecox'* Funnel-shaped flowers in open clusters, purple-crimson in bud, opening to rosy purple, produced late winter to early spring. Foliage can be slightly deciduous, yellow older leaves contrasting with dark glossy green new leaves; aromatic when crushed. *R. racemosum* Funnel-shaped flowers, pale to bright pink, produced in axillary buds, forming racemes along branches. Foliage oblong to elliptic, leathery-textured with blue glaucous undersides. In favourable conditions may exceed mature height and spread. *R. saluenense* Clusters of rose-purple to purple-crimson, funnel-shaped flowers in mid to late spring. A mat-forming shrub with very thick, grey-green, aromatic foliage, ovate to elliptic. Reaching only one-third mature height and spread. *R. williamsianum* Shell pink, bell-shaped flowers in early spring, round, heart-shaped leaves. Can exceed mature height and spread. *R. yakushimanum* Trusses of large, bell-shaped flowers borne in late spring, rose-pink in bud, opening to apple blossom pink, eventually aging to white. Dark, glossy green foliage, curving at edges with brown-blue undersides.

Average height and spread
Five years
2x2ft (60x60cm)
Ten years
2½x3ft (80cmx1m)
Twenty years or at maturity
3x5ft (1x1.5m)

ROBINIA Pink-flowering forms

FALSE ACACIA
Leguminosae
Deciduous
Attractive late spring-flowering trees, not well known and
deserving more attention.

Origin South-western USA; some named
varieties from France.
Use As large shrubs or small trees for flowering display. Ideal for all sizes of garden. Can
be fan-trained on to a large wall if required, a
procedure which shows off the flowers to best
advantage.
Description *Flower* Clusters of pea-flowers,
up to 3in (8cm) long on wood two years old or
more, in early summer. *Foliage* Pinnate
leaves, up to 6in (15cm) long with 9-11 oblong

Robinia kelseyi
in flower

or ovate leaflets each 2in (5cm) long. Light
grey-green with yellow autumn colours. *Stem*
Light grey-green to grey-brown with small
prickles. Upright when young, spreading and
branching with age. Branches and twigs
appear dead in winter, but produce leaves
from apparently budless stems in late spring.
Grown as large shrubs or as single-stemmed
trees. *Fruit* Small, grey-green, bristly pea-
pods, up to 4in (10cm) long, in late summer
and early autumn.
Hardiness Tolerates 14°F (−10°C) but stems
may suffer some tip damage in severe winters.
Soil Requirements Most soil conditions; parti-

cularly tolerant of alkaline types. Resents waterlogging.

Sun/Shade aspect Full sun to very light shade.

Pruning None required. Young shoots can be shortened in early spring to encourage strong regrowth but this curtails flowering.

Propagation and nursery production From seed or grafting. Purchase container-grown. Normally available from 5-8ft (1.5-2.5m). Best planting heights 5-6ft (1.5-2m). Must be sought from general or specialist nurseries; most varieties not offered by garden centres.

Problems Notorious for poor establishment; container-grown trees provide best results. Branches may be damaged by high winds and need shelter.

Varieties of interest *R*. × *ambigua* Light pink flowers. Pinnate leaves with 13-21 light grey-green leaflets. Must be sought from specialist nurseries. *R. 'Casque Rogue'* Rose-pink to pink-red flowers. An interesting variety from France. Difficult to find. *R. fertilis 'Monument'* Possibly best grown as a large suckering shrub, but can be encouraged to produce a single stem. Rosy red flowers. Half average height and spread. From south-eastern USA. *R*. × *hillieri* Slightly fragrant lilac-pink flowers. Originally raised in Hillier's Nurseries, Hampshire, England. *R. kelseyi* Flowers bright purple-pink. Attractive pale grey-green foliage with 9-11 leaflets. From south-eastern USA. Must be sought from specialist nurseries. *R. luxurians* Rose pink flowers. Leaves up to 12in (30cm) long, pinnate and with 15-25 oval bright green, leaflets. Slightly more than average height and spread. Not readily available; must be sought from specialist nurseries. From south-western USA.

Average height and spread
Five years
10x6ft (3x2m)
Ten years
20x13ft (6x4m)
Twenty years or at maturity
39x20ft (12x6m)

SENECIO

SHRUBBY RAGWORT
Compositae
Evergreen
Attractive, silver-leaved shrubs with white or yellow daisy-like summer flowers.

Origin From New Zealand.

Use As a low, grey foliage shrub for front of shrub borders. Effective for mass planting. Planted 2ft (40cm) apart makes low informal hedge.

Description *Flower* Clusters of yellow, daisy-shaped flowers in early summer, maintained over long period. *Foliage* Leaves ovate, 1-2½in (3-6cm) long, sometimes cut-leaved, silver-grey. *Stem* Upright, becoming branching and spreading with age. Grey. Slow to medium growth rate. *Fruit* Insignificant.

Hardiness Tolerates 14°F (−10°C).

Soil Requirements Well-drained, open soil, dislikes waterlogging.

Sun/Shade aspect Full sun to very light shade.

Pruning Trim lightly each spring to keep shrub healthy. Once growth starts, old woody shrubs can be cut back hard in early spring,

Senecio 'Dunedin Sunshine' in flower

and will rejuvenate from ground level.

Propagation and nursery production From semi-ripe cuttings taken early to mid summer. Purchase container-grown. Best planting heights 1-1½ft (30-50cm).

Problems Can become woody, but an annual trimming as suggested should prevent this.

Varieties of interest *S. cineraria* (Dusty Miller, Silver Groundsel) Very white, felted, cut-leaved foliage, surmounted by yellow daisy-shaped flowers in summer. Many named varieties offered as annuals for bedding rather than as permanent shrubs, but in areas where temperature does not fall below 23°F (−5°C) may be considered hardy. *S. compactus* Small, ovate, wavy-edged grey-green leaves with white undersides. Young shoots and flower stalks are also white-felted. Bright yellow daisy-shaped flowers produced early to mid summer. Dislikes waterlogging. Low-growing variety. Tender and should not be subjected to frost. *S. 'Dunedin Sunshine'* syn. *S. laxifolius* Ovate, silver-grey foliage surmounted by daisy-shaped flowers in terminal panicles. Can become woody without adequate pruning. In addition to trimming, one-third of oldest wood should be cut back to ground level in spring to induce new growth. *S. greyi* Very downy, soft grey foliage. Yellow flowers in summer. Tender and should not be subjected to forst. Scarce. *S. hectori* Leaves grey-green with white undersides and toothed edges. Semi-evergreen. Clusters of white flowers, mid to late summer. Needs protection, minimum winter temperature 23°F (−5°C). May be hard to find. *S. leucostachys* Very lax growth covered with very finely divided silver-white pinnate leaves, covered with good-sized white, daisy-shaped flowers throughout summer. From Patagonia. *S. monroi* Oblong or oval leaves, dark steel grey with wavy curling edges. Flower spikes and

Average height and spread
Five years
2½x2½ft (80x80cm)
Ten years
3x3ft (1x1m)
Twenty years or at maturity
3x5ft (1x1.5m)

72

young shoots grey to white felted. Terminal clusters of yellow daisy-shaped flowers. Reaches two-thirds average height and spread. *S. reinoldii* syn. *S. rotundifolia* Large, round, leathery, dark grey-green, glossy foliage. Terminal round, open clusters of yellow daisy flowers in summer and early autumn. Minimum winter temperature 23°F (−5°C). In favourable conditions reaches 6ft (2m) height and spread.

SPIRAEA Low-growing varieties

KNOWN BY BOTANICAL NAME
Rosaceae
Deciduous
Attractive, small, low shrubs for late spring and early summer flowers.

Origin From the Himalayas, through China and Japan.
Use For front of large shrub-borders, for mass planting, or for low hedge if planted 1¼ft (40cm) apart.
Description *Flower* White, pink or pink-red clusters of flowers, depending on variety, in midsummer. *Foliage* Leaves ovate, 1-3in (3-8cm) long, often tooth-edged, mainly light to dark green; some golden-leaved forms. Some good autumn colour in all varieties. *Stem* Short, very branching and twiggy, forming round-topped mound. Fast growth rate when young, slowing with age. *Fruit* Insignificant, but brown seedheads of winter interest.
Hardiness Tolerant of winter temperatures down to −13°F (−25°C).
Soil Requirements Most soils, disliking only extremely alkaline or dry types.

Spiraea × *bumalda* '*Anthony Waterer*' **in flower**

Spiraea × bumalda
'Gold Flame' **in leaf**

Sun/Shade aspect Prefers full sun, tolerates light to medium shade.

Pruning According to variety. Most of those listed in this section merely need thinning by removing one-third of oldest flowering wood in early spring, to encourage rejuvenation. Some other varieties should be cut to ground level, as recommended below.

Propagation and nursery production From semi-ripe cuttings taken early to mid summer. Purchase container-grown. Most varieties easy to find, especially when in flower. Best planting heights 1¼-2ft (40-60cm).

Problems No real problems if pruned correctly; otherwise can become woody.

Varieties of interest *S. albiflora* syn. *S. japonica alba* Light green lanceolate foliage with coarsely-toothed edges and glaucous green undersides. Clusters of fluffy-textured white flowers borne at ends of branches, midsummer. Thin wood by one-third in spring. From Japan. *S. × bumalda 'Anthony Waterer'* New foliage occasionally appears pink and cream variegated, but not as a general rule. Leaves are ovate, tooth-edged, dark green with a reddish hue along the veins. Bright clusters of dark pink-red flowers are produced in early to mid summer. Should be cut to ground level early each spring to encourage good foliage and maximum flowering performance; if just thinned it will achieve more height and spread but have smaller flowers. *S. × b. 'Gold Flame'* New foliage in spring orange-apricot, becoming orange-red and finally gold. May be scorched in strong sunlight. Dark pink-red flowers in early to mid summer. Should be reduced to ground level in early spring to encourage rejuvenation of attractive growth and large flowers. *S. japonica 'Bullata'* syn. *S. crispifolia, S. bullata* Very small, broad, ovate leaves, deeply veined, dark grey-green with lighter undersides. Flowers small, dark crimson, produced in flat clusters in midsummer and presented well above the dark foliage. No pruning required. Reaches two-thirds average height and spread. *S. j. var. fortunei* syn. *S. j. wulfenii* Foliage incised and tooth-edged purple-green-red with glabrous undersides. Very attractive. Rich dark pink flowers in midsummer. Branches may be thinned or pruned back hard. From Europe and central China. *S. j. 'Golden Princess'* Small mounds of golden yellow foliage, susceptible to scorching by strong summer sun, early to mid summer. Thin wood lightly in spring. *S. j. 'Little Princess'* A dwarf, low, spreading carpet of light green, tooth-edged foliage, surmounted by rose-crimson flowers in midsummer. Thin wood lightly in spring. *S. 'Shirobana'* Interesting light green to mid green, tooth-edged leaves. Flowers, either pink, all white, or half pink, half white, make an interesting flowering combination in early summer. May be thinned or cut back hard in spring. Of garden origin.

Average height and spread
Five years
1¼x1½ft (40x50cm)
Ten years
2x2¼ft (60x70cm)
Twenty years or at maturity
2x2¼ft (60x70cm)

Spiraea 'Shirobana' in flower

SYRINGA Cultivars

LILAC
Oleaceae
Dedicuous
One of the most spectacular groups of large scented shrubs for late spring or early summer-flowering.

Origin All varieties of garden origin; many were raised by Victor Lemoine and his son Emile in their nurseries in Nancy, France at the turn of the century. Alice Harding, author of the definitive book on this genus, was also responsible for a large number of varieties in production today.

Syringa 'Primrose'
in flower

Use As freestanding, flowering shrubs, either singly or in groups. Ideal for mass or specialist planting, also as background planting for larger shrub borders. Can be planted 3ft (1m) apart in single line to make an attractive, informal low hedge or screen. Also sometimes obtainable as small mop-headed standard on stem 5-6ft (1.5-2m) high.

Description *Flower* Large single or double florets in large fragrant panicles, in colours ranging from blue to lilac, through pink to red or purple, to white or yellow, with some bicoloured forms. Late spring, early summer. Colour, size of shrub, degree of fragrance and flowering time dependent on variety. *Foliage* Leaves dark green to mid green, medium-sized, ovate, 2-6in (5-15cm) long and 1¼-2½in (3.5-6cm) wide. *Stem* Stout shoots, grey-green to grey-brown with pronounced buds, either green-yellow or red-purple, depending on variety, in winter. Forms an upright, conical shrub; may form a small multi-stemmed tree after 10-15 years. Fast growth rate when young, slowing with age. *Fruit* Grey-brown seedheads maintained into winter.

Hardiness Tolerant of winter temperatures down to −13°F (−25°C).

Soil Requirements Most soils, but may show signs of chlorosis on severely alkaline types.

Sun/Shade aspect Prefers full sun, tolerates up to medium shade.

Pruning Requires very little pruning, but remove dead seedheads in winter to increase flowering. Old stems and unwanted suckers can be removed as necessary. Cutting back hard reduces flowering in next 2-3 years.

Propagation and nursery production From budding or grafting using either *S. vulgaris*, *Ligustrum vulgare* or *L. ovalifolium* as under-stocks. Can also be raised from semi-ripe cuttings taken early to mid summer. Best purchased container-grown, but can also be planted bare-rooted or root-balled (balled-and-burlapped). Availability varies. Best planting heights 2-3ft (60cm-1m).

Problems Often planted in areas where full growth potential is restricted. Young plants may take up to 3-5 years after planting to come into full flower.

Varieties of interest *Single-flowered varieties:* *S. 'Congo'* Large panicles of rich, lilac-red flowers in mid to late spring, becoming paler with age. Must be sought from specialist nurseries. *S. 'Etna'* Flowers rich purple to claret red, late spring to early summer, aging to lilac-pink. Must be sought from specialist nurseries. *S 'Firmament'* Flowers mauve in bud, opening to clear lilac-blue, mid spring. A very free-flowering variety. *S. 'Lavaliensis'* Very attractive pale pink flowers. Smaller than average, bright green foliage. Slightly less than average height and spread. Difficult to find. *S. 'Marechal Foch'* Panicles of bright crimson-rose flowers in mid spring. Must be sought from specialist nurseries. *S. 'Massena'* Large, broad panicles of deep red-purple flowers in late spring, early summer. Must be sought from specialist nurseries. *S. 'Maud Nottcutt'* Very stately panicles of white flowers in mid spring. One of the best single-flowering varieties, good for flower-arranging material. *S. 'Night'* Very dark purple flowers in mid spring. May be hard to find. *S. 'Primrose'* Pale primrose yellow to yellow-white flowers in mid spring. A dense, compact shrub. *S. 'Reamur'* Large panicles of deep red-purple flowers, shaded with violet, in early summer. Must be sought from specialist nurseries. *S. 'Sensation'* Large panicles of purple to purple-red, white-edged florets in mid to late spring. Flower variegation may be lost in some seasons. A shrub of loose, open habit. Must be sought from specialist nurser-

Syringa 'Souvenir de Louis Spaeth' **in flower**

Syringa 'Madame Lemoine' in flower

ies. *S. 'Souvenir de Louis Spaeth'* Large, broad trusses of wine red flowers in mid to late spring. A strong-growing shrub of spreading habit. *S. 'Vestale'* Large, loose panicles of pure white flowers, in mid to late spring. Light green foliage. Compact habit. ***Double-flowering varieties: S. 'Belle de Nancy'*** Lilac-pink flowers opening from purple-red buds in mid spring. *S. 'Charles Joly'* A very dark red-purple form. Large flower panicles produced in late spring, early summer. *S. 'Edward J. Gardner'* Large semi-double, light pink flowers, in mid spring to late spring. *S. 'Kathleen Havermeyer'* Wide, tight flower panicles, purple-lavender, becoming paler lilac-pink, in late spring, early summer. *S. 'Madame A. Buchner'* Semi-double, mauve-shaded rose-pink florets in feathery flowerheads. Very good scent. Tall, open growth habit. *S. 'Madame Lemoine* Large white flower panicles in mid spring. A large, wide, round shrub, one of the most popular forms. *S. 'Michel Buchner'* Pale rose-lilac flowers in dense panicles, very fragrant, in late spring. A large, upright shrub. *S. 'Mrs. Edward Harding* Semi-double, purple-red, fragrant flowers in mid to late spring. Tall-growing, open habit. *S. 'Paul Thirlon'* Deep rose-red flowers in late spring, early summer. May be difficult to find; should be sought from specialist nurseries. *S. 'Souvenir d'Alice Harding'* Large panicles of soft white flowers in late spring, early summer.

Average height and spread
Five years
4x3ft (1.2x1m)
Ten years
8x5ft (2.5x1.5m)
*Twenty years
or at maturity*
16x10ft (5x3m)

SYRINGA × JOSIFLEXA 'BELLICENT'

CANADIAN LILAC
Oleaceae
Deciduous
Given space, a true treasure of a flowering shrub for the larger garden.

Origin Raised in Ottawa, Canada in the early 1900s.
Use As a freestanding, specimen shrub, or as background planting for large shrub borders.
Description *Flower* Large, fragrant panicles, up to 10in (25cm) long and plume-like, of clear rose pink, open flowers; slightly arching in display. *Foliage* Leaves ovate, 4-6in (10-15cm) long and 2-3in (5-8cm) wide. Very dark green and attractive, giving some yellow autumn colour. *Stem* Upright when young, spreading with age and forming a wide-topped, narrow-based shrub. Stout, upright branches infrequently producing side shoots at low levels, branching more towards ends. Grey-green to grey-brown. Fast growth rate when young, slowing with age. *Fruit* Old seedheads, grey-brown, may be retained well into winter if not removed as advised.
Hardiness Tolerates winter temperatures down to −13°F (−25°C).
Soil Requirements Most soils but distressed by chlorosis on alkaline types.

Syringa × josiflexa
'Bellicent' **in flower**

Average height and spread
Five years
4x3ft (1.2x1m)
Ten years
10x6ft (3x2m)
*Twenty years
or at maturity*
16x13ft (5x4m)

Sun/Shade aspect Full sun to light shade.
Pruning Remove one-third of oldest shoots biennially to induce rejuvenation on established shrubs more than 5 years old. Seedheads should also be removed as soon as seen.
Propagation and nursery production By budding, or from semi-ripe cuttings taken in early summer. Purchase container-grown, bare-rooted or root-balled (balled-and-burlapped). Best planting heights 2-3ft (60cm-1m).
Problems Young plants can look stunted and lopsided, but grow rapidly once planted. Often planted in areas which restrict full growth potential.

VIBURNUM PLICATUM

DOUBLEFILE VIBURNUM, JAPANESE SNOWBALL, LACECAP VIBURNUM
Caprifoliaceae
Deciduous
Extremely attractive snowball or lacecap-flowering spring shrubs in a wide range of sizes.

Origin From Japan and China.
Use For small, medium or large shrub borders, according to variety. For mass planting or as individual specimens.
Description *Flower* Either globular snowball heads of white florets, or flat, lacecap, hydrangea-like flowers with central fertile small flowers, surrounded by white ray florets. Both types produced late spring, early summer. *Foliage* Leaves 2-4in (5-10cm) long, ovate, with pleated effect and pronounced channelling along veins, light to mid green. Some good autumn colour, particularly after a dry summer or in very dry soils. *Stem* Upright when young, quickly becoming spreading to form dome-shaped, wide shrub.

Viburnum plicatum
'Mariesii' in flower

Light green to green-grey. Can spread to extent of producing flat tiers of growth, a habit common to all but more pronounced in some varieties. Medium growth rate. *Fruit* Clusters of oval, red to red-orange fruits in autumn, on mature shrubs more than 5 years old on relatively dry to average soil. Fruiting can be erratic.

Viburnum plicatum
'Pink Beauty'
in flower

Hardiness Tolerates 4°F (−15°C).
Soil Requirements Tolerates wide range of soils but extremely waterlogged or dry areas will damage its fine-textured root system.
Sun/Shade aspect Prefers light shade, tolerates from full sun to medium shade.
Pruning None required.
Propagation and nursery production From semi-ripe cuttings taken in early summer or from layers. Purchase container-grown or root-balled (balled-and-burlapped). Most varieties fairly easy to find. Best planting heights 1¼-3ft (40cm-1m).
Problems Very susceptible to root damage, from cultivation such as hoeing, or from extreme drought or waterlogging. If roots are damaged, a section of top growth will die back. In severe cases this can destroy the shrub completely.
Varieties of interest *Lacecap flowering varieties: V. plicatum 'Cascade'* Large, white flat flowers. Fertile inner small tufted florets, surrounded by a ring of bold white ray florets. Red fruits after hot summer. Large, ovate, pointed foliage, giving good autumn colour, on branches arching to give semi-weeping effect. Less likely to die back than other varieties. Two-thirds average height and spread. *V. p. 'Lanarth'* White, large, flat, lacecap flowers produced in defined tiers along horizontal branches. Large, ovate, mid to dark green foliage, giving good autumn colour. Sometimes listed as shorter growing shrub; initially when this variety was cata-

Viburnum plicatum
'Watanabe' in flower

logued it was confused with *V. p. 'Mariesii'*,
'Lanarth' being described as the lower of the
two varieties, but the reverse is the case. *V. p.*
'Mariesii' White lacecap flowers borne on
very horizontal, tiered branches. Good fruiting with fine autumn colour. Reaching half
average height and spread. *V. p. 'Pink Beauty'*
Ray florets of white lacecap flowers, aging to
attractive pink. Small to medium, ovate, dark
to olive green foliage. Good autumn colour.
Two-thirds average height and spread. *V. p.*
'Rowallane' White lacecap flowers in late
spring. Small, ovate, tooth-edged foliage,
mid to dark green, giving some autumn tints.
Closely tiered branch effect. Extremely reliable fruiting form. May be more difficult to

Viburnum plicatum
'Grandiflorum'
in flower

find than most. Two-thirds average height and spread. *V. p. var. tomentosum* Flowers 2-4in (5-10cm) across, creamy white and surrounded by white ray florets, giving way to red, oval fruits, which age eventually to black. Bright green, pleated, ovate foliage. Good autumn colour. Not easy to find. From Japan, China and Taiwan. *V. p. 'Watanabe'* syn. *V. semperflorens* Very compact, producing good-sized white lacecap flowers in early summer through to mid autumn. Some orange-red fruits, late summer through to autumn. Reaching only two-thirds average height and spread. *Snowball flowering varieties: V. macrocephalum* Semi-evergreen. White, round, large, globular heads of sterile flowers, 2¾-6in (7-15cm) across, late spring. Medium-sized, ovate foliage, light green, up to 2-4in (5-10cm) long. Somewhat less hardy than most, requiring a favourable sunny position on a wall in areas where temperature falls below 23°F (−5°C). Extremely difficult to obtain, but not impossible. *V. plicatum 'Grandiflorum'* (Japanese Snowball) Large, round to globular, sterile heads of white florets. New flowerheads in spring attractive green, aging to white, taking on pink margin and finally overall pink towards end of flowering period in midsummer. Foliage large, ovate, mid green tinged purple. Good autumn colour. Must have good moist soil and light dappled shade to do well; resents full sun. Two-thirds average height and spread.

Average height and spread
Five years
8x6ft (2.5x2m)
Ten years
12x10ft (3.5x3m)
Twenty years or at maturity
16x16ft (5x5m)

VIBURNUM Spring-flowering, scented forms

KNOWN BY BOTANICAL NAME
Caprifoliaceae
Deciduous and Semi-evergreen
Some of the most highly scented of spring-flowering shrubs.

Origin Basic forms from Korea, with many garden hybrids.
Use As fragrant spring-flowering, medium-sized shrubs for planting individually, in groups, or in medium to large shrub borders. Many forms do well in containers over 2ft (60cm) in diameter and 1¼ft (40cm) in depth; use good quality potting medium. Occasionally obtainable as short, mop-headed standards and can be used as feature planting.
Description *Flower* Medium to large, round, full clusters, consisting of many tubular flowers, varying shades of pink to white in early to late spring. All highly scented. *Foliage* Leaves ovate, medium-sized, 2-4in (5-10cm) long, grey-green, some yellow autumn display. *Stem* Upright, covered with grey scale when young, becoming branching to form dome-shaped shrub. Medium growth rate. *Fruit* May produce blue-black fruits in autumn.
Hardiness Tolerant of 4°F (−15°C).
Soil Requirements Most soils, disliking only very dry or very wet types.

Sun/Shade aspect Prefers light shade, accepts full sun to medium shade.

Pruning None required, but remove any suckering growths appearing below graft or soil level.

Propagation and nursery production Normally from grafting on to an understock of *V. lantana*. Some varieties from semi-ripe cuttings taken in early summer. Purchase container-grown or root-balled (balled-and-burlapped). Best planting heights 2-3ft (60cm-1m). Most varieties fairly easy to find, especially when in flower. Particular varieties and standard forms may have to be obtained from specialist nurseries.

Problems All forms, particularly *V. carlesii* and its varieties, suffer from aphid attack. Root systems of all forms are very fibrous and surface-rooting and react badly, sometimes succumbing completely, to damage caused by cultivation drought or waterlogging.

Varieties of interest *V. bitchiuense* (Bitchiu Viburnum) Clusters of pink, scented flowers, mid to late spring. Foliage ovate to elliptic, dark metallic green. Open habit. From Japan. *V. × burkwoodii* (Burkwood Viburnum) Clusters of pink buds open into fragrant, white tubular flowers, early to mid spring. followed by clusters of blue-black fruits. Semi-evergreen ovate foliage with dark green, shiny surface. As leaves die off in autumn they turn scarlet, red and orange, contrasting with remaining dark green foliage. Forms large round-topped shrub or can be fan-trained as a wall shrub. Reaches one-third more than average height and spread. *V. × b. 'Anne Russell'* Semi-evergreen. Large clusters of pale pink, fragrant flowers in mid spring, dark pink in bud. *V. × b. 'Chenaultii'* Semi-evergreen. Flowers similar to *V. × burkwoodii*, but does not reach same overall proportions. Not easy to find. Two-thirds

Viburnum ×
burkwoodii **in flower**

average height and spread. ***V.* × *b.* 'Fulbrook'**
Large white flowers, pink in bud and sweetly
scented. ***V.* × *b.* 'Park Farm Hybrid'** A form
with larger, more vigorous habit of growth.
Flowers, mid spring, slightly larger than the
form. Good glossy green foliage. ***V.* × *carl-
cephalum*** A deciduous variety producing
large, white, tubular florets, pink in bud, very
fragrant. Complete clusters are 4-5in (10-
12cm) across and extremely attractive. Large,
ovate to round, grey-green foliage, may produce good autumn colours. ***V. carlesii***
(Koreanspice Viburnum) Clusters of pure
white, tubular flowers, opening from pink
buds, with strong scent, in mid to late spring.
Ovate to round, downy, grey to grey-green
leaves with grey felted undersides, producing
good red-orange autumn colouring. Some
forms of *V. carlesii* are weak in constitution
and named varieties may be more successful.
***V. c.* 'Aurora'** Red flower buds, opening to
fragrant pink tubular flowers produced in
clusters, mid to late spring. Good ovate
grey-green foliage. Good constitution. ***V. c.*
'Charis'** Good, vigorous growth. Flowers red
in bud, opening to pink and finally fading to
white. Very good scent. Foliage clean and
grey-green. May be difficult to find, but not
impossible. ***V. c.* 'Diana'** A good clone of
compact habit. Flowers pink, red in bud.
Good fragrance. May be difficult to find but
not impossible. ***V.* × *juddii*** (Judd Viburnum)
Clusters of scented, pink-tinted tubular
flowers, produced at terminals of branching
stem, mid to late spring. Grey-green ovate
foliage with some autumn colour. Open in
habit when young, becoming denser with age.
Two-thirds average height and spread.

**Average height
and spread**
Five years
3x3ft (1x1m)
Ten years
5x5ft (1.5x1.5m)
*Twenty years
or at maturity*
6x6ft (2x2m)

WEIGELA

KNOWN BY BOTANICAL NAME
Caprifoliaceae
Deciduous
Shrubs for late spring and early summer-flowering.

Origin Most forms from Japan, Korea, North China and Manchuria, but many cultivars and hybrid varieties are of garden origin.

Use As a freestandiing shrub on its own or as mid to background shrub for shrub borders. If planted 2½ft (80cm) apart in single line, makes flowering, informal hedge. Can be fan-trained, especially the variegated forms, for use on cold, exposed or shady walls. Small mop-headed standards on 5-5½ft (1.5-1.8m) high stems are obtainable, mainly in the red-flowering forms.

Description *Flower* Funnel-shaped, good-sized flowers in varying shades from yellow, through white, to pink and red. Flowers produced on wood 2 years old or more, late spring through early summer, possibly with intermittent flowering through late summer and early autumn. *Foliage* Leaves ovate, 1½-5in (4-12cm) long, dark to mid green with some light green varieties and golden and silver variegated. Some yellow autumn colour. *Stem* Upright, becoming spreading with age. Grey-green to grey-brown. Medium growth rate. *Fruit* Seedheads dark to mid brown, of some attraction in winter.

Hardiness Tolerates −13°F (−25°C).

Soil Requirements Any soil.

Sun/Shade aspect Prefers full sun, tolerates light to medium shade.

Pruning From two years after planting, remove one-third of old flowering wood annually after flowering to encourage rejuvenation and good production of flowering wood.

Weigèla florida
'Foliis Purpureis'
in flower

Weigela florida
'Albovariegata' **in leaf**

Propagation and nursery production From semi-ripe cuttings taken in early summer or hardwood cuttings in winter. Purchase container-grown. Most varieties easy to find, but some may have to be obtained from specialist nurseries. Best planting heights 1¼-2½ft (40-80cm).

Problems If unpruned can become too woody and flowers will diminish in size and number. Large, established shrubs can be cut to ground level and will regenerate, but will take two years to come into flower. *Weigela* was once classified with the closely related *Diervilla* but in recent years these shrubs have been classified separately.

Varieties of interest *W. florida 'Albovariegata'* Attractive creamy white edges to ovate leaves. Pale to mid pink flowers produced profusely on stems 2 or 3 years old. Useful as wall climber for cold, exposed walls. Two-thirds average height and spread. *W. f. 'Aureovariegata'* A variety with yellow variegation, often producing pink to red tinged leaves, particularly during autumn. Pink flowers profusely produced in late spring to early summer. Useful as wall shrub for cold, exposed walls. *W. f. 'Foliis Purpureis'* Attractive purple-flushed leaves produced in spring, which age and become duller as summer progresses. Purple-pink flowers in late spring, early summer. Not widely enough planted. One-third average height and spread. *W. middendorffiana* Arching branches with attractive grey-green winter wood. Flowers bell-shaped, sulphur yellow with dark orange markings on lower lobes, mid to late spring. Ovate, light green foliage with some yellow autumn colour. Prefers light shade, although not fussy. An all-round, attractive variety, reaching two-thirds average height and spread. From Japan, Northern China and Manchuria. *W. praecox 'Variegata'* A variety with ovate to obovate, creamy white variegated foliage, rigid and deeply veined. Flowers honey-scented, rose pink with yellow

Weigela 'Bristol Ruby' in flower

markings in throat, late spring, early summer. Obtain from specialist nurseries. From Japan, Korea and Manchuria. **Weigela cultivars and hybrids:** *'Abel Carrière'* Large, trumpet-shaped, rose-carmine flowers with gold markings in throat, opening from purple-carmine buds. Good, bold, green foliage. *'Avalanche'* A good, strong-growing, white flowering variety. May have to be obtained from specialist nurseries. *'Boskoop Glory'* Large, trumpet-shaped, salmon-pink flowers. A beautiful form. Two-thirds average height and spread. *'Bristol Ruby'* Possibly the most popular of all flowering forms. Ruby red flowers profusely borne on upright, strong shrub in late spring, early summer. *'Candida'* Pure white flowers with slightly green shading.

Weigela 'Candida' in flower

Light green foliage on arching stems. Two-thirds average height and spread. *'Eva Rathke'* Bright crimson-red flowers with yellow anthers, produced over long period from late spring until late summer. *'Looymansii Aurea'* Flowers pale pink, contrasting with foliage which is light golden yellow in spring aging to lime-yellow in autumn. Must be in light shade or it scorches. Obtain from specialist nurseries. Often looks weak when young. One-third average height and spread. *'Mont Blanc'* Fragrant white flowers, strong-growing. Obtain from specialist nurseries. *'Newport Red'* Good, dark red flowers. Two-thirds average height and spread. *'Stelzneri'* Good mid pink flowers borne in profusion. Interesting upright growth. Not widely available, but not impossible to find. *'Styriaca'* Carmine-red flowers produced in good quantities in late spring, early summer. Strong, very old-fashioned variety.

Weigela 'Looymansii Aurea' in flower

Average height and spread
Five years
4x4ft (1.2x1.2m)
Ten years
5½x5½ft (1.8x1.8m)
Twenty years or at maturity
7x7ft (2.2x2.2m)

PLANTING TREES AND SHRUBS

Successful establishment of a tree or shrub begins with the important stage of preparing a correctly sized planting hole. The planting process may seem somewhat laborious, but it is worthwhile providing the best conditions, as a tree or shrub may be the focal point of the garden and can give years of pleasure if allowed to establish itself properly.

Preparing the planting hole

The diameter and depth of the planting area depends upon the size of a tree or shrub, as follows:

For trees up to 9ft (2.8m) when purchased, the planting hole should be 3ft (1m) in diameter. For trees up to 16ft (5m), the required size is 4½ft (1.4m) or more.

The depth of preparation is the same for trees of all heights – 18in (50cm). The soil is worked over in two stages: planting depth corresponds to the original depth of soil around the tree or shrub, but a similar depth of soil is broken up and prepared below the actual planting depth.

Remove the topsoil to a depth of 9in (25cm). Store the soil on a flat board beside the planting hole and add to it half a bucket of compost or well-rotted farmyard manure.

Fork over and break up a further 9in (25cm) of subsoil. Remove any weed roots from the soil as it is turned. Dig in half a bucket of compost or well-rotted farmyard manure.

For shrubs reaching an ultimate height of not more than 18in (50cm), the minimum diameter of the planting hole should be 2ft (60cm). For shrubs which will ultimately exceed this height, the required size of planting hole is 3ft (1m).

The depth of prepared planting area is the same in both cases, 18in (50cm); soil preparation is in two stages as described above for trees.

Planting container-grown shrubs or trees

A container-grown tree or shrub should be well-watered before it is planted, ideally at least one hour beforehand.

Place the plant, still in its container, in the planting hole and adjust the depth so the rim of the container is just below the surrounding soil level. The container can now be removed, taking care not to disturb the soil ball around the roots of the plant.

Never lift the plant by its trunk or stems, as this can tear and damage the roots. Handle the whole root ball carefully and once the container has been removed, take care that small exposed roots do not dry out.

Replace the prepared topsoil around the root ball of the plant to the level of the soil around the planting hole. Tread the soil gently all around the plant to compress it evenly. Unless the soil is very wet, pour a bucket of water into the depressed area.

Fill the area with more prepared topsoil, bringing the level up just above that of the surrounding soil. Dig a small V-shaped trench, 3in (8cm) deep and wide, around the planting area to allow drainage.

Planting bare-rooted trees or shrubs
The basic planting method is the same for bare-rooted or root-balled (balled-and-burlapped) plants as for container-grown, but it is even more important that the roots should not be allowed to dry out. When returning the topsoil to the planting hole, take care to work it well in around the roots of the tree or shrub, leaving no air pockets in the soil.

Staking a tree
A young tree should be staked as soon as it is placed in the planting hole. The stake should be at least 1-1½in (3-4cm) thick, round or square-sectioned with a pointed tip, and treated to resist rotting. Select a suitable length to support the height and weight of the tree – the top of the stake should extend well into the upper stems or branches, and the point should go into the subsoil to a depth of 18in (50cm).

When the tree is in place in the planting hole, push the stake through the soil ball and into the prepared subsoil below. If it meets a definite obstruction, remove the stake and try in a different spot, but not more than 2in (5cm) from the tree stem.

To support the tree, fasten two adjustable ties, with small spacing blocks to hold the tree clear of the stake, one on the stem among the branches as high as is practical, the other halfway up the main stem or trunk.

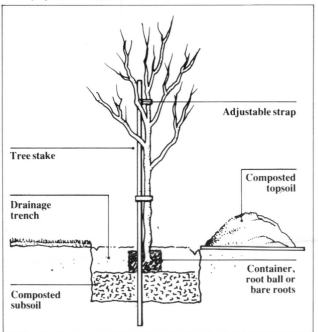

Adjustable strap

Tree stake

Drainage trench

Composted topsoil

Composted subsoil

Container, root ball or bare roots

Planting times – UK and Europe

Bare-rooted or root-balled trees or shrubs can be planted at any time from late autumn to early spring, except in the harshest of winter conditions. Do not plant when the ground is frozen or waterlogged.

Container-grown trees or shrubs can be planted at any time of year, unless weather conditions are extreme. Do not plant when the ground is frozen, dried hard, or waterlogged.

Planting times – USA

Plant bare-rooted trees and shrubs in late winter or early spring, just before bud break. Bare-rooted trees and shrubs lose most of their root surface – and water-absorbing capacity – during transplanting. New roots will not develop until spring, so if you plant in fall, there is the risk that buds and twigs will dry out over winter.

Fall is the best time to plant balled-and-burlapped and container-grown trees and shrubs, because it gives them a long season of cool air and warm soil for strong root growth. Roots put on most of their year's growth after leaf-fall.

Planting times – Australia and New Zealand

Bare-rooted trees or root-balled trees or shrubs can be planted at any time from late autumn to early spring, unless the ground is frozen hard or waterlogged.

Container-grown trees and shrubs can be planted at any time of year unless weather conditions are extreme. Do not plant when the ground is frozen, dried hard or waterlogged or when conditions are extremely hot and dry.

PRUNING

Pruning cuts
It is important to cut a stem at the correct angle when pruning, at a point slightly above a bud with the cut sloping away from it at a gentle angle (below).

Correct pruning of a tree or shrub can improve and increase the plant's flowering and fruiting, the size and colour of foliage, and the appearance of attractive stems and bark. It controls and shapes the growth of the tree or shrub, so that it remains an attractive garden feature suited to the location where it is growing.

All trees and shrubs should be inspected every spring for broken twigs and branches and other signs of damaged wood, which is not only unsightly but also vulnerable to disease. Soft or woody growth which has suffered winter die-back should also be cut back in spring. Trees frequently develop crossing branches which may rub together and cause a lesion that may become the site of various diseases; this also occurs in shrubs, but less commonly. The weaker of the two branches should be removed in winter, or while the plant is dormant.

Methods of pruning
There are some slow-growing trees and shrubs which require no pruning, while others

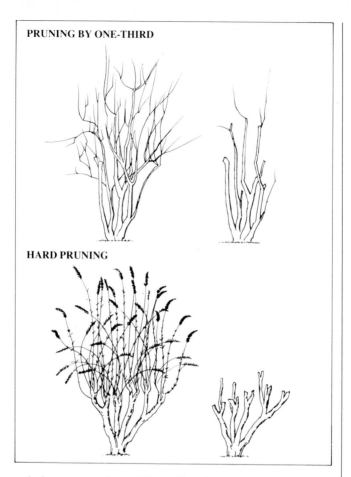

PRUNING BY ONE-THIRD

HARD PRUNING

actively resent pruning and if cut will tend to die back. It may also be inadvisable to prune if this will remove flower buds at the terminals of twigs or branches. Otherwise, a plant can be lightly trimmed or pruned back hard, or one-third of the growth may be selectively removed to encourage new growth production.

Many shrubs gain improved flowering performance in the coming season if all growth is cut back to ground level in mid to late spring. The shrub will rapidly rejuvenate and there is no advantage to pruning less severely where cutting right back is recommended. Hard pruning is slightly less drastic, consisting of cutting back all growth to new growth points on woody stems near the plant base.

Another method of encouraging better flowering is to remove one-third of the oldest growth or old flowering wood as soon as the flowering period has ceased. One-third of old growth is removed in spring of the first year; in the following spring, another one-third of the mature wood, and again in the third year when the last of the old growth is removed.

INDEX OF LATIN NAMES

INDEX OF COMMON NAMES